One to Watch, One to Pray

by

Minka Shura Sprague

Library of Congress Cataloging-in-Publication Data

Sprague, Minka Shura.
One to Watch, One to Pray.

1. Bible. N.T. Gospels—Criticism, interpretation,
etc. 2. Bible. N.T. Gospels—Authorship. I. Title.
BS2555.2.S66   1988   226'.06   87-28279
ISBN 0-8192-1452-3

Printed in the United States of America
by
BSC Litho

for Chuck,
"One to Heal" in his own time
and the Angel of the
Church of the Holy Trinity

Contents

Introduction

Matthew, Mark, Luke and John,
Guard the bed I lie upon.
Four pillars round my bed;
Four angels round my head.

One to watch, one to pray,
And two to keep me till the day. Amen.

As a child, this was my first prayer. With this prayer, I "grew up," and moved from the fertile farmland of Missouri to Minnesota, then to Ohio, finally to New York City. With this prayer woven into the tapestry of my soul, I sacramentalized relationships, bore children, took my words into advertising and onto community playhouse stages and into editorial columns of local newspapers. With this prayer woven into the tapestry of my soul, I fell into seminary and did a first degree and some continuing education and an advanced degree in New Testament. I was forty years old, and on the home stretch of General Seminary's Th.D. when my childhood prayer began to shine through the tapestry of my soul.

This is a book about the New Testament Gospels—the four stories of Jesus that the early church found most valuable, valuable enough to name and claim as "Holy Scripture." And this is a book about the authors of the Gospels—the anonymous "men" we call Matthew, Mark, Luke and John. On these pages, I sketch the shapes of the Gospels, their similarities and their differences. On these pages, I tell a story of how they came to be written, how they are related to each other, something of how and why these stories of Jesus have always been at the heart of the faith of the Church of God. This is a book to read as we read the Gospels, alone and in community.

Lent was well on its way when I realized that my childhood prayer provided the shape and the name and something of the value of my adult education series in St. Michael's and Holy Trinity Episcopal Churches. In each case, the Lenten program was titled "The Evangelists." Holy Week was almost in view before I could feel the effect of the childhood prayer, before I found the words with which I had gone to sleep for so many years.

One to Watch, One to Pray is my story about the Gospels and my childhood prayer. But the story that is to come belongs, first of all, to the faithful followers who wrote the stories of Jesus—Matthew, Mark, Luke and John.

And then this story belongs to the Family of God, a chosen people for 200 generations, a Christian people for the last two thousand years. This is our story, our family, our people—and in this I rejoice, for this I pray, Amen.

Minka Sprague
Holy Trinity Episcopal Church, New York City
Ash Wednesday, 1986

Chapter 1

"Four Angels Round My Head"

We begin in prayer, asking the authors of our Gospels to be our guardians. "Four pillars round my bed; four angels round my head" are the words of our prayer. This is a little startling. We are not accustomed to thinking about the authors of our Gospels in this way. More often, we think of Matthew, Mark, Luke and John as "the Evangelists," or "saints" of the Church of God. Indeed, we do have "guardian angels" in the Christian tradition, and their names are Gabriel, Michael, Uriel and Raphael. What does it mean to think of "the Evangelists" as the "four angels round my bed?"

Christian art is full of angels. When we imagine angels, we see the angels portrayed by Byzantine, medieval and Renaissance artists. They tend to have haloes and wings; they wear long, flowing dresses and are ethereal other worldly creatures. If we are to find meaning for our prayer, we must travel back before these artists' time. We must ask what the authors of our Gospels meant by the word "angel," what "angel" would have meant in Jesus' time.

When we ask these questions, we find ourselves in the first century and we discover that we must turn to the Old Testament for understanding. When Jesus or the authors of our Gospels refer to "the Scriptures," they refer to our "Old Testament." In the first century, we are in the time before "the New Testament," a time before the term "Christian." In the first century, our people are the Hebrew people of God, the Jewish chosen people. And we discover that our people have a long history with "angels."

We also discover that while our people are a Hebrew people, we encounter our history with "angels" in the Greek language. In the first century, Greek is the language of the Roman Empire. It is the language that the world uses to do its business across cultural boundaries. The New Testament documents are all written in the Greek language. Jesus probably spoke Aramaic in the countryside of Judea and Galilee and worshipped in Hebrew in the synagogue and temple. Had he traded in the coastal cities of Tyre and Sidon, however, he would have spoken Greek. By the first century, the Hebrew Scriptures had existed in a widely-accepted Greek translation for more than two hundred years.

The word "angel" is a Greek word that means "one who is sent" or "messenger." An "*angelos* of the Lord" is often God's messenger in the Old Testament stories. Think of the "messengers" that come to Abraham and Sarah, for example, or the "angel" with whom Jacob must wrestle for his life. These stories are the holy tradition that lives in the hearts and on the souls of the authors of our Gospels. It is not surprising, therefore, to find "messengers of the Lord" in our New Testament as well. For instance, Luke tells us that an "*angelos* of the Lord" comes to Zechariah, that "the *angelos* Gabriel was sent by God" to Mary. (Luke 1:11,26)

In both our Old and New Testaments, an angelos can

be a human or a divine envoy. The "messengers" that Jesus sends into Samaria to prepare his way are human ones. (Luke 9:52) But most of the "angels" we meet are sent by God. These "messengers" come from God and return to God; they appear and suddenly disappear. They bear "messages" that are good news or shocking news or specific divine instructions. Sometimes, their "messages" are in physical acts instead of spoken words. In the book of Acts, for example, an "angel of the Lord" releases Peter from prison. (Acts 5:19) And in Matthew's story of the resurrection, there is an earthquake " . . . for an angel of the Lord descended from heaven and came and rolled back the stone and sat upon it." (Matthew 28:2)

Whatever their appointed task or message, "angels of the Lord" bring God into relationship with the world. This relationship with God occurs in a single event, a one-time occurrence. An "angel of the Lord" sharpens communication between God and the People of God. In a moment, whether it be in action or in words, God's "messenger" brings creation and her Creator close. The "angel" is the connecting link between creation and Creator. The "angel" serves as the matrix through which conversation may occur, the matrix through which relationship is known.

The "angels" are the way in which God communicates with the People of God on special occasions. As a Hebrew people, we related to God on a day-to-day basis through the Law and our prophets. In the light of the resurrection, we know God and are known by God in every moment of every day through the power of the Holy Spirit. But when communication needs to be sharpened, or there is something special to say or do,

God sends "angels", divine "messengers." We may imagine these "angels" with outstretched arms, holding God with one hand and those to whom God comes in the other. In the stories of our people, this has always been the case. In special times, we have held the hands of the "angels" so that we could touch God.

Can we, then, think of Matthew, Mark, Luke and John as "angels," as God's "messengers"? Each of our Evangelists was sent by God at a special time to a particular community with a special task. And each of our Gospels draws the People of God into closer relationship with God. Each of our Gospels sharpens the communication between God and the People of God. Each of our Gospels serves as the connecting link between creation and her Creator. Indeed, it is only through our Gospels that we are able to reach the stories of Jesus at all. Matthew, Mark, Luke and John each had a particular "message" from God for their own communities in their own time. Whether each of the Evangelists knew this or not, each of these "messages" lived on with meaning and with truth long after the community and the author were gone. Matthew, Mark, Luke and John are the "angels" whose hands we hold when we reach out to touch Jesus. The authors of our Gospels offer us their hands as we reach out to be in closer relationship to God.

When we touch the hands of our "four angels," we remember that they are human at the same time that they are God's "messengers." Our Christian tradition has given our Gospels the names of men, so we presume that the hands that we hold are masculine ones. They are Jewish hands as well, for each of our "angels" is a faithful follower of Jesus and God's "messenger" within the context of Judaism. Were these hands fleshly rather than figurative hands, we would look for color and feel for age and weather-beaten lines. As it is, we hold each of our "angels' " hands through their words.

We began with words of prayer, asking our "angels" to be our guardians. With our words of prayer, we reach out to their words—the words of the Gospels—as we ask them to be "one to watch, one to pray, and two to keep us until the day." Amen.

Chapter 2

"In the Beginning Was the Word"

Each of our four Gospels begins uniquely and from each of the Gospel introductions, we learn a great deal. This is where we first learn something about the author's intentions, something about the literature itself and something about who Jesus is according to the author's point of view.

Matthew, the author of our first Gospel, calls his work "the book of the genealogy of Jesus Christ, the Son of David, the son of Abraham." Our first Gospel is a *biblion*, the Greek word that we recognize in English words like "Bible" and "bibliography."

Our second Gospel has a very different introduction. This is, says Mark, "The beginning of the gospel of Jesus Christ, the Son of God." The word for "gospel" is not a description of literature at all; *euanggelion* means "good news", and this is the word from which we get the religious terms "evangelist" and "evangelism." But it is also from Mark's introduction that the church has come to think of the stories of Jesus as "Gospels", as *euanggelia*. Mark's use of the word *euanggelion* changed literature in western civilization for all time. It called a new type of literature into being, one in which the story of Nazareth was told in such a way as to allow the faithful family of God to carry on God's work in the world.

The author of our third Gospel knows and says that he is writing literature. He has a proper literary introduction, so hang onto your seat. When Greek writers of the first century have proper literary intentions and proper literary introductions, *we* get very long sentences. Here is the lengthy one-sentence introduction to Luke: "Inasmuch as many have undertaken to compile a narrative of the things which have been accomplished among us, just as they were delivered to us by those who from the beginning were eyewitnesses and ministers of the word, it seemed good to me also, having followed all things closely for some time past, to write an orderly account for you, most excellent Theophilus, that you may know the truth concerning the things of which you have been informed." What a mouthful. "Others have written narratives," Luke tells us. "Mine, however, is an 'orderly account' and you can trust it."

A "book," a "gospel" and an "orderly account"— Matthew, Mark and Luke. What have we from the fourth Gospel, the Gospel of John? We have no explanation or title at all. Here, instead, is what we have: "In the beginning was the Word, and the Word was with God, and the Word was God. He was in the beginning with God; all things were made through him, and without him was not anything made that was made. In him was life, and the life was the light of mankind. The light shines in the darkness and the darkness has not overcome it."

There is no title, no name, no introduction at all. John's "In the beginning . . . " of the fourth Gospel pushes the one who hears or the one who reads these words all the way back in time, beyond time, beyond creation. John claims that for as long as there has been time and space and life and creation, Jesus has existed with God, as God—God, the Creator of the universe, God whom Jesus calls "the Father."

"In the beginning was the *logos*," says John. And John's readers would know this *logos*, this "word" to be a for-all-time divine creative energy, a force and power of the universe. "You want to know who Jesus is?" asks the author of the fourth Gospel. "I'll tell you who Jesus is. Jesus is the *logos*, the Word." John continues: "And the Word became flesh and dwelt among us, full of grace and truth; we have beheld his glory, glory as of the only Son of the Father . . . and from his fullness have we all received, grace upon grace. For the law was given through Moses, grace and truth came through Jesus Christ. No one has ever seen God; the only Son who is in the bosom of the Father, he has made him known."

John's gospel, John's story of Jesus of Nazareth as the *logos* was written for our faithful forebears, a community that lived and loved and worshipped and prayed in the third generation in the light of the resurrection. We are the 100th generation of the faithful followers of Christ in the light of the resurrection. This is the figure one gets if one takes 2000 years and thinks of a generation as twenty years and then does long-division, old-fashioned mathematics.

There are good reasons for thinking of ourselves in faithful generations, and they have to do with who we are as the People of God and what it is we are to do as God's family. The first of these reasons is that our family stories in the Old Testament tell us that God thinks of the Chosen People in generations. God's promise came to Abraham, and to the generations that would follow him. And the apostle Paul reminds us that we are sons and daughters of Abraham. We are the 200th generation of the Chosen People, the People of God led up from slavery out of Egypt.

And then, since God thinks of us in generations, we can be sure that God is committed to the creation and the life of all creation for *all* time. We are God's people in this span of all time that can only be imagined in God's mind. We are called to live and love and work in our time in God's creation—always for justice, and as often as it is possible, with joy. Thinking of ourselves in generations gives us an opportunity to share that joy. Too often, preachers use "it has been 2000 years since Christ" to suggest that the People of God have failed entirely. Implicit in this remark is the suggestion that God's people are responsible for the consummation and perfection and coming-to-an-end of all creation. And we are not. We are to see that there is justice in the creation—that the poor are not hungry, that the marginalized are cared for, that the prisoners are set free. We are to love God and our neighbors as ourselves. We are to celebrate our anniversaries as the People of God, and we are to let God be God as Creator and Redeemer of the universe in which we find ourselves.

Our name is the Chosen People, the People of God. And this name describes us not as individuals, but as a collective, corporate, communal body. As God's people, we were led into the Promised Land, taken in and out of exile, and given a messiah in answer to our prayers. As a people, we have been given the power of the Holy Spirit.

The Holy Spirit is incredibly unique. Never in the

New Testament does the Spirit fall upon or is poured
out upon an individual. The Holy Spirit is *always*
poured out upon two or more who are gathered together. This means that in the light of the resurrection,
the Holy Spirit always relates the faithful to each other
at the same time it relates the faithful to God. There is
no other spirit or power or principality or energy or god
in the Greek or Hebrew world that behaves like this. As
we become God's children in the power of the Holy
Spirit, we also become sisters and brothers in the Family of God.

We can know ourselves as this people, this family
only if we claim and value all our generations—our suc-
cesses and our failures, our high points and our low
ones, the times we recognize and to which we relate and
those to which we cannot.

As Christians, we have our people in a number of
different traditions, some which go back to Henry VIII,
some which go back to Luther or Calvin, some which
go back to Jan Hus and so forth. And as Christians, we
have a catholic tradition that stretches back across time
and space into the very first communities of the faithful
who told the stories of Jesus, and celebrated "He is
Risen!" as the truth.

And then we have our people in the Scriptures. Our
people sang Zion's songs in a foreign land and then at
home in Judea. Our people gave us Amos' basket of
summer fruit and Jeremiah's despair and Ruth's love
for Naomi and Moses' sermons and Jonah's willful dis-
obedience. Our people followed Jesus from Galilee
down into Judea, shouted "Crucify him!" and wept at
the foot of his cross. Our people were the congregations
for whom Paul wrote. And our people gave us a

"book" called Matthew, a "gospel" called Mark, an "orderly account" called Luke, and these words: "In the beginning was the Word . . . "

Beginnings happen with words, and with the Word—in words and with words and with the Word of God in Scripture and with Jesus, the Word became flesh—because *this* is the way we relate to God and to each other. This is why we read and discuss Scripture over and over again. This is why it is never enough to say "I love you" only once. In the light of the resurrection, in the life of God's people, there are never too many words. Words must be dreamt and read and shouted and whispered and debated and sometimes even taken back. As the Bible is the Word of God, written in the voices of God's people, so too our words carry God's energy, God's power, the presence of God's Holy Spirit. It is our task and our call and our gift that we are so chosen. And thank God, we have the words of our forebears with which to walk and worship.

There is no way for us to know exactly how the words of our New Testament Scriptures were collected and arranged; exactly how this happened is known only to God. But we do know this: It is the eighth or so generation of Christianity in southern France, and ecstatic Christian groups are frankly running away with the church. There is little if any agreement about who and what Jesus is, who and what the Holy Spirit is, how and what faithful followers are to do with their lives or with each other or with their Scriptures. The Scriptures at this time are the Hebrew Scriptures, just as they were for Jesus, and the earliest generations of faithful followers of Christ. The Christian "scene" is on of confusion; it is a mess.

One of our bishops takes a hard look at this "scene" and gasps in dismay. In response, he commissions Irenaeus, Bishop of Lyons, to write a book that will address and solve some of these problems. Irenaeus takes the job and writes a book called *Against Heresies*.

From *Against Heresies*, we can tell two very important things about the collection of Christian writings that we will someday call the "New Testament." First of all, in 170 A.D., Irenaeus has almost exactly the same collection of Gospels and Epistles that we have today. His collection does not have 1-2 Timothy and Titus, and it does have something called "The Sheperd of Hermas." Not only does Irenaeus seem to have most of what we call the "New Testament;" it is also pretty much in the same order that we know it today. It looks like Irenaeus' collection of Christian writings goes like this: Matthew, Mark, Luke, Acts, Romans, 1 Corinthians and so on.

The second thing that we can tell from *Against Heresies* is that Irenaeus is the person who gets the Gospel of John into the New Testament. When we read Irenaeus, we can tell that the Gospel of John is part of the problem. Further, we can tell that while Irenaeus knows that this is the case, he can also envision the Gospel of John as the solution. The fourth Gospel is the story of Jesus that the ecstatic Christian communities like the very best. "Wait," Irenaeus says, "don't let them have it. It is a fine Gospel. Indeed," he goes on to say, "it is precisely the Gospel that we need for the upbuilding of the Church of God. We *must* have the Gospel of John, too."

Irenaeus expects an argument from the church about the Gospel of John. And we can tell this because he gets in his own argument before his opposition gets the chance. He begins by saying that it is not the fourth Gospel's fault that it is misinterpreted and misused. This is Irenaeus' way of saying that the problem is *not* that the fourth Gospel is "unorthodox." The problem, says Irenaeus, is that unorthodox Christians are using a perfectly good story of Jesus.

Then Irenaeus goes on to give his own particular reasons for inclusion of the fourth Gospel in the Christian canon of writings. "We only have three Gospels now," he says. "It is not a complete set. We need four Gospels." And before his reader can ask the obvious question, Irenaeus answers, "There are four elements of the universe—wind, fire, earth and water. There are four corners of the world. There are four winds and four seas. There must be four Gospels." He insists, "Add the Gospel of John." And so we did.

The good news is that we got a complete set of Gospels. The bad news is that our faithful forebears did not put in the Gospel of John at the front of the Christian writings. This would have made sense. The Gospel of John begins with the words, "In the beginning . . . " and it could have well been the beginning. Maybe our forebears simply did not think of this. Maybe our faithful forebears already had their own version of our prayer that begins "Matthew, Mark, Luke . . . " For whatever reason, the Gospel of John was added as the fourth Gospel, and was dropped into the middle of the two-volume work we know as Luke-Acts.

Irenaeus was right, of course. Think how impoverished we would be without the fourth Gospel. It has always been called "the spiritual Gospel" and it is the Gospel that sits in the soul of every Christian generation. He was also right about the "complete set." Four *is* the number of completion. Three is a tense number, a configuration that embraces and contains tension, a configuration through which energy pulses and moves. This is why the Christian doctrine of the Trinity has been creative and powerful throughout our 100 generations. This is why triangles architecturally support flying buttresses. This is why the Gospels of Matthew, Mark and Luke also remain as a powerful, energetic collection of the stories of Jesus.

Sometimes the pulsating, never-ending energy of triangles and trinities needs to be relieved or completed. So Irenaeus argued, and so the New Testament came to include the Gospel of John.

A "book," a "gospel," an "orderly account," and the bold claim: "In the beginning was the Word and the Word was with God and the Word was God . . . " Or in other words, "Matthew, Mark, Luke and John, guard the bed I lie upon. One to watch, and one to pray . . . " As always, prayer is proper for "In the beginning . . . " and it is to the "One to Pray" that we now turn.

Chapter 3

"One to Pray"

The fourth Gospel is the most familiar, best loved and most different of the New Testament Gospels. Since about 250 A.D., John has been called "the spiritual Gospel." In the Middle Ages, amulets with words from the fourth Gospel were worn for protection from evil and disease. The beginning of John's Gospel was traditionally read as "the final Gospel" at the close of the Roman mass until recent times. To this very day, John's story of Jesus sits on the hearts and souls and rises to the lips of the faithful first. It is the Gospel the church has always taken into prayer. Of our four angels, our four Gospels, John is our "One to Pray."

Matthew, Mark and Luke are the Gospels that are closely related to each other; they are like siblings or first cousins. John is also related to this trinity of Gospels, but as a distant kinsperson, a cousin once or twice "removed." And it is precisely what is different in John that is familiar to the faithful.

Only John has the bold claim that Jesus is the *logos*, the Word made flesh. It is from John that we think of Jesus as the good shepherd, the light of the world, the bread of life, the true vine, the way and the truth and the life. When we recall Jesus' ministry of miracle, we think of him raising Lazarus from the dead or changing the water into wine at the wedding in Cana. These pieces of tradition belong to John alone.

It is in John that Jesus washes the disciples' feet. Only in John do we discover that "there was much grass" at the feeding of the multitudes. Nathanael's ironic question about Jesus comes from John: "Can anything good come out of Nazareth?" And only the Gospel of John has the author's signature at the end. "This is the disciple," our author writes, "who is bearing witness to these things and who has written these things, and we know that his testimony is true." (John 21:24)

Now—aside from someone who says that he can be trusted, just who is this author? How are we to glimpse his understanding of God's action in history in the life and death and resurrection of Jesus? John writes for the nurturing and upbuilding of the faithful community. How might we glimpse this community? "John," the author of our Gospel, is a messenger, and "angel" who bears the Word of God to all faithful Christian generations. In our time, we want to hold John's hand, to receive his message.

We begin by reaching out to him, to his Gospel as a whole. First of all, we examine the shape, the outline, the structure of the book in its entirety. Those of us who encounter the Gospels in worship rarely have an opportunity to do this. And we are so accustomed to reading and hearing the Gospels in sayings and phrases and short readings that it never occurs to us to examine one whole book at a time. But these sayings and stories all have their own literary contexts. They all "fit" somewhere else—in a chapter, in a collection of stories or sayings, in a literary unit within the book. Each of them allows us a glimpse of a larger story. Like pieces of a jigsaw puzzle, they are part of a larger picture. The shape of this larger picture can tell us something about the author's message for us, as well.

Each of the Gospels has two parts to the story of Jesus. In each of the Gospels, part of the story tells of Jesus' ministry and part of the story tells of Jesus' arrest and trial and crucifixion—the events that the church has come to know as the "passion" of Christ. And in each of the Gospels, the story shifts from the account of the ministry to the account of the passion with Jesus' triumphal entry into Jerusalem. This is one way in which all four Gospels are alike. From this point, however, all four Gospels are very different. Matthew, Mark, Luke and John each have a shape to their story that is uniquely their own.

The Gospel of John has a shape that is almost perfectly balanced between the story of Jesus' ministry and the story of his passion. And as we recall, John is both the most different of the Gospels and the last one to become part of the New Testament, to become "Holy Scripture." For this reason, John's very balanced shape is probably not a coincidence. Since John is the last of our four Gospels to be written, it is altogether probable that our author has considered such things. Luke's introduction tells us that he knows of other "narratives" about Jesus. And if John is the last of our four Gospels, it is more than probable that he knows these as well, and his intentions could have included the balancing of this two-part story.

When we look at the outlines of the fourth Gospel, we discover that it divides neatly in half. An outline of its content looks like this:

1:1-18	"The Prologue" ("The *Logos* Hymn")
1:19-11:54	The Ministry of Jesus (Gospel of Signs)
11:55-20:31	The Passion of Jesus (Farewell Discourses)
21:1-25	Conclusion

This outline can also be nicely diagrammed and looks like this:

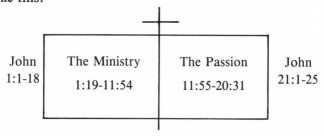

| John 1:1-18 | The Ministry 1:19-11:54 | The Passion 11:55-20:31 | John 21:1-25 |

This particular shape of the Gospel of John emerges when we look at the book from a couple of different perspectives. In two ways, the content of the material tells us that we have moved from one place to another, from one section to another. The "*Logos* Hymn" ends in 1:18 and "the testimony of John" begins a new piece of the story in 1:19. The author summarizes the effects of Jesus' raising of Lazarus in 11:45-54, closing with "Jesus therefore no longer went about openly among the Jews, but went from there to the country near the wilderness, to a town called Ephraim, and there he stayed with the disciples." A new section begins abruptly with "Now the Passover of the Jews was at hand . . . "

This means that the story line tells us something of the shape of the book. And this becomes even more obvious if we read the Gospel in the English translation of the text known as the Revised Standard Version. The editors of the RSV translation of the New Testament put spaces between 1:18-19 and 11:54-55 to show the reader that there are spaces here in the Greek text. And these spaces in the Greek text tell us that the author of our Gospel *also* thinks that this is where a new section begins.

Once we allow the story line and the divisions in the text to tell us about the shape of the Gospel, we suddenly see that in the first half of John, there is a lot of talk about "signs" and that the references to "signs" end abruptly in Chapter 12. In the second half, Jesus makes long speeches that we have *not* seen before Chapter 12, and there is no talk of "signs" in this second half at all.

Questions tumble forth once we see the "signs" in the story of Jesus' ministry and the long speeches in the story of his passion. Matthew, Mark and Luke do not have either this talk about "signs" or these long speeches from Jesus. What is John's message in these "signs" and speeches? We discover that the fourth Gospel is a complicated piece of literature with an interesting story to tell.

"Signs," *semeia*, are to the Greeks of John's time what they are for us today, with the exception of billboards. To the best of our knowledge, the invention of billboards comes later than the time of the Roman Empire. "Signs" point the way toward something. A *semeion* is the characteristic by which someone or something may be known. And then, for the Greeks who really believed that God intervened in the events of history, the events of humanity and the universe, "signs" signify the intervention of a more-than-human power, good or bad. In the first half of our Gospel, this is what "signs" do. In John, the *semeia* are good. They

belong to Jesus and they signify the intervention of God
in Christ Jesus in the events and affairs of those people
whom Jesus encounters. Further, Jesus' "signs" all
have a result; they point the way to belief, to faith.

For John, Jesus' public ministry begins in Chapter 2,
with the marriage at Cana in Galilee, where Jesus turns
the water into wine. Our author summarizes this event
in v. 11: "This, the first of his *signs*, Jesus did at Cana
in Galilee, and manifested his glory; and his disciples
believed in him."

John continues his narrative, telling us that it is the
time of the Passover and that Jesus went up to Jerusalem for the feast. Here, he drives the money-changers
from the temple. This is his first confrontation with the
religious establishment and those who witness his au-
thoritative act challenge Jesus, asking him, "What *sign*
have you to show us for doing this?" (2:18) In v. 23, the
author summarizes the event: "Now when he was in
Jerusalem at the Passover feast, many believed in his
name when they saw the *signs* which he did."

Jesus is again in Cana in Galilee when we next hear
of his "signs." While there, an official from Capernaum comes to him and asks him to heal his dying son.
Jesus responds to his request with "Unless you see *signs*
and wonders you will not believe." (4:48) The official
beseeches Jesus, who then promises, "Go; your son will
live." John tells us that the official believed Jesus and
"went his way." (4:49-50) Then he summarizes the
event: "The father knew that that was the hour when
Jesus had said to him, 'Your son will live'; and he himself believed, and all his household. This was now the
second *sign* that Jesus did when he had come from
Judea to Galilee." (4:53-54)

In Chapter 6, we have John's version of Jesus' feeding of the multitude, and again, the author summarizes his account with a statement of the people's belief. "When the people saw the *sign* which he had done, they said, 'This is indeed the prophet who is to come into the world.' "(6:14) Following the feeding of the multitude, Jesus and the disciples start across the Sea of Galilee to Capernaum. Jesus' followers witness his walking upon the sea, experience fear, receive Jesus' reassurances and take him into the boat. On the next day, John tells us, the people follow Jesus to the other side of the sea. Again, there is conversation between Jesus and the people that results in confrontation with the religious establishment. The people begin by asking Jesus how he reached the other side of the sea. Jesus replies with "Truly, truly, I say to you, you seek me, not because you see *signs*, but because you ate your fill of the loaves. Do not labor for the food that perishes, but for the food which endures to eternal life, which the Son of Man will give to you; for on him has God the Father set his seal." They ask him what they are to do, and Jesus tells them that they are to believe in the one whom God has sent. Their reply to Jesus' insistence upon their faith is a challenge: "Then what *sign* do you do that we may see and believe you?" they respond. (6:26-30)

When Jesus heals the man who is born blind, confrontation is once again the result. Here, the religious establishment debates the issue among themselves. Some of them say, "This man is not from God, for he does not keep the Sabbath." But others say, "How can a man who is a sinner do such *signs*?" And John tells us that "there was a division among them." (9:16)

Jesus does no "signs" in the following chapter, yet

even his words cause the confrontation to which we are now accustomed. So John tells us with the following: "There was again a division among the Jews because of these words. Many of them said, 'He has a demon, and he is mad; why listen to him?' Others said, 'These are not the sayings of one who has a demon. Can a demon open the eyes of the blind?' " (10:19-21) And John summarizes the entire chapter with this: "[Jesus] went away again across the Jordan to the place where John at first baptized, and there he remained. And many came to him, and they said, 'John did no *sign*, but everything that John said about this man was true.' And many believed in him there." (10:40-42)

In John's story, a crisis is building between those who witness Jesus' "signs" and teaching. We can hear the crescendo of this crisis in the aftermath of Jesus' raising Lazarus from the dead. In 11:45, John tells us that many who witness this event believe in Jesus, but others go to the Pharisees and tell them what Jesus has done. The religious establishment gathers to discuss the issue. "What are we to do?" they ask. "For this man performs many *signs*. If we let him go on thus, every one will believe in him, and the Romans will come and destroy both our holy place and our nation." (11:47-48)

We can almost hear an hysterical tone under John's words. Those who are threatened by Jesus' "signs" and his teaching seem to be desperate about what it is they should do. They need a solution to the problem. And it is Caiaphas, the high priest of the year, who offers the solution. " . . . It is expedient for you," he says, "that one man should die for the people, and that the whole nation should not perish." And John tells us that "from that day on they took cousel how to put him to death." (11:50-53) We have not quite reached the middle of John's Gospel, and the die is cast.

In the center section of the Gospel, we are reminded that Jesus' fate has been sealed. Jesus has spent some time with Mary, Martha and Lazarus and has entered Jerusalem triumphantly. A crowd goes out to meet him, and waving palm branches, they cry, "Hosanna! Blessed is he who comes in the name of the Lord, even the King of Israel!" (12:13) John tells us that the reason the crowd goes to meet Jesus is because they had heard of the raising of Lazarus, " . . . they heard that he had done this *sign*." Those who have religious power reassure themselves that they have interpreted the events correctly and that they are moving on the right course of action. They say to one another, "You see that you can do nothing; look, the whole word has gone after him." (12:18-19) With Jesus' triumphal entry into Jerusalem, we have moved into John's second half of the Gospel, his story of Jesus' passion. Our author refers to the controversy in belief that Jesus' words and "signs" have caused one last time in Chapter 12. "Though he had done so many *signs* before them, yet they did not believe in him," John writes and attributes this to the hardness of heart and blindness prophesied in Isaiah 6:10 and Isaiah 53:1. "Nevertheless," our author concludes, "many even of the authorities believed in him, but for fear of the Pharisees they did not confess it, lest they should be put out of the synagogue." (12:37-42)

We have reason to believe that John has inherited these stories of Jesus' "signs," and that he has incorporated them into the fourth Gospel as we know it today. We can see this when we look at all the references to "signs" in the Gospel without looking at the au-

thor's comments *upon* them. We have just completed
looking at the "signs" material this way. And we have
discovered that Jesus' "signs" and the controversy that
they cause have two results. The first is always that
someone or several people believe in Jesus because of
the "signs" he does. The second result is that the belief
that Jesus' "signs" cause controversy and a division
among the people. Because of this controversy and division, the religious establishment decides to have Jesus
killed. The story of Jesus' "signs" ends in the center of
the fourth Gospel, just as he enters into Jerusalem, her-
alded by the people as the "king of Israel."

Within the text, what does our author have to say
about this? The author's comments that stand out like
neon signs are Jesus' "I am . . . " statements. There
are seven of these familiar statements in the fourth Gospel. Five of these "I am . . . " statements occur in the
story of Jesus' ministry, the story of Jesus' "signs"
through which we have just walked. A chart of John's
references to Jesus' "signs" and Jesus' "I am . . . "
statements looks like this:

2:11		"the first of his signs" and belief
2:18		"what sign do you show?"
2:23		"many believed . . . when they saw"
4:53-54		"he believed . . . this was the second sign"
6:14		" . . . saw the sign . . . this is the prophet"
6:26		"you seek me not because you saw signs"
6:30		"what sign do you do?"
	6:35	"I am the bread of life"
	8:12	"I am the light of the world"
9:16		"how can . . . a sinner do such signs?"
	10:7	"I am the door of the sheep"
	10:11	"I am the good shepherd"

10:41-42	"John did no sign . . . many believed"
11:25	"I am the resurrection and the life"
11:45-47	"many believed . . . this man performs many signs"
12:18	"the crowd went . . . he had done this sign"
12:37-42	"though he had done so many signs, they did not believe . . . many even of the authorities believed in him."

In each of the five cases, the "I am . . . " saying goes a step past the events or discussions that surround the "signs." In each instance, the "I am . . . " statement insists that the belief that comes from seeing Jesus' "signs" is not enough. With each "I am . . . " saying, Jesus suggests that faith is more than "seeing is believing." It is as if Jesus says, "Now that you have seen that, believe *this* . . . " or "If you have seen that and believe, then *know* this to be true and believe."

In among the stories of Jesus' "signs," our author comments upon "seeing is believing" and says, "This, too, must be said." He does this for several reasons. The first is that for John, this story about Jesus' "signs" explains why the religious authorities were so threatened that they must have Jesus killed. All of our Gospels must address this question one way or another, and the answer is never an obvious one. Jesus had a life-giving proclamation and a life-giving ministry. Why murder such a man? John's answer is that precisely because of this ministry and these "signs," the religious authorities were afraid that "the world has gone after him." (12:19)

The second reason John adds the "I am . . . " sayings to the "signs" material is that they point the way to the second half of the Gospel, the story of Jesus'

passion. The five "I am . . . " sayings in the first half
of the Gospel are the way in which Jesus will teach his
disciples in the final time before his death. For John,
the raising of Lazarus signals the end of Jesus' public
ministry, the end of Jesus' ministry of miracle. From
his entry into Jerusalem forward, Jesus spends his time
with his followers, teaching them over and over, "*This
is who I am* . . . " And the first five "I am . . . "
sayings show John's reader how this will be.

We may suppose that there is a third reason as well.
John's Gospel comes to us in its present form from the
turn of the first century. John's community is nearly
seventy years away from the death and resurrection of
Christ. This is, as we figure it, three generations later.
The faithful followers who actually witnessed Jesus'
"signs" are no longer around to tell how they saw the
unbelievable and believed. Indeed, those to whom they
entrusted their stories and their faith are gone as well.
John knows that "seeing is believing" must be followed
by "knowing is believing" if the truth is to be made
known. John knows that his community must know
who Jesus is in order to believe. "This is who Jesus is,"
John writes for his reader. "This is who I am." Jesus
says.

John's story of the passion begins in Chapter 12
when Jesus rides into Jerusalem amid the palm
branches. As we have seen before, John shares much of
his version of these events with the other three Gospels.
At the same time, we may also say that his account is
the most unique. Nowhere else do we hear of Thomas,
and there is a footwashing instead of "the last supper."
The inscription on the cross occurs in three languages
and Nicodemus accompanies Joseph of Arimathea in

the burial. Even the shape of John's passion is different from the other Gospels, and this is what concerns us here.

John takes the last events of Jesus' life and wraps them around Jesus' "This is who I am . . . " teaching with his disciples. When we look at it carefully, we can see that it is actually like a sandwich. The events of Chapter 12 and 13 make up one slice of bread. These are: the triumphal entry into Jerusalem (12:12-19); the footwashing (13:1-20); the foretelling of the betrayal and the denial (13:21-38). The betrayal, Jesus' arrest and trial, the crucifixion and burial and one set of resurrection appearances make up the other slice of bread. These events begin in 18:1 and end with the story of "doubting Thomas" in 20:29. The filling of this sandwich is found in Chapters 14-17, Jesus' "This is who I am . . . " teaching with the disciples. It is rich fare indeed.

This teaching is often referred to as the "Farewell Discourses," and it is here that we find the two remaining "I am . . . " sayings. The first of these occurs at the beginning of the section, just after the foretelling of the betrayal and the denial. Jesus begins with reassurances. "Let not your hearts be troubled;" he says in 14:1. "Believe in God, believe also in me." He promises that he will bring the disciples where he is going, and says that they know the way. Thomas asks, "Lord, we do not know where you are going; how can we know the way?" Jesus replies, "I am the way, and the truth, and the life . . . " (14:5-6)

Again, there are reassurances from Jesus. "These things I have spoken to you, while I am still with you," he says. "But the Counselor, the Holy Spirit, whom the

Father will send in my name, he will teach you all things and bring to your remembrance all that I have said to you." (14:25-26) And we find the last of our "I am . . . " sayings on the heels of this promise. "I am the true vine, and my Father is the vinedresser," Jesus says to his followers, using the agricultural image to talk of his relationship to God and their relationship to him. These relationships are characterized as "abiding," lasting, enduring. "You did not choose me, but I chose you," Jesus says, "and appointed you that you should go and bear fruit and that your fruit should abide; so that whatever you ask the Father in my name, he may give it to you. This I command you, to love one another." (15:1,16-17)

Jesus completes his teaching with a final reassurance. "I have said this to you, that in me you may have peace," he says. "In the world you have tribulation; but be of good cheer, I have overcome the world." (16:33) Jesus then turns to his Father in prayer.

The words of John 17 are the right words with which to close, since John, of our four authors, of the "four angels round my head," is the "one to pray."

John 17

> When Jesus had spoken these words, he lifted up his eyes to heaven and said, "Father, the hour has come; glorify thy Son that the Son may glorify thee, since thou has given him power over all flesh, to give eternal life to all whom thou hast given him. And this is eternal life, that they know thee the only true God, and Jesus Christ whom thou hast sent. I glorified thee on earth, having accomplished the work which thou gavest me to do; and now, Father, glorify thou me in thy own presence with the glory which I had with thee before the world was made.

"I have manifested thy name to the men whom thou gavest me out of the world; thine they were, and thou gavest them to me, and they have keep thy word. Now they know that everything that thou hast given me is from thee; for I have given them the words which thou gavest me, and they have received them and know in truth that I came from thee; and they have believed that thou didst send me. I am praying for them; I am not praying for the world but for those whom thou hast given me, for they are thine; all mine are thine, and thine are mine, and I am glorified in them. And now I am no more in the world, but they are in the world, and I am coming to thee. Holy Father, keep them in thy name, which thou hast given me, that they may be one, even as we are one. While I was with them, I kept them in thy name, which thou hast given me; I have guarded them, and none of them is lost but the son of perdition, that the scripture might be fulfilled. But now I am coming to thee; and these things I speak in the world, that they may have my joy fulfilled in themselves. I have given them thy word; and the world has hated them because they are not of the world, even as I am not of the world. I do not pray that thou shouldst take them out of the world, but that thou shouldst keep them from the evil one. They are not of the world, even as I am not of the world. Sanctify them in the truth; thy word is truth. As thou didst send me into the world, so I have sent them into the world. And for their sake I consecrate myself, that they also may be consecrated in truth.

I do not pray for these only, but also for those who believe in me through their word, that they may all be one; even as thou, Father, art in me, and I in thee, that they also may be in us, so that the world may believe that thou hast sent me. The glory which thou hast given me I have given to them, that they may be one even as we are one, I in them and thou in me, that they may become perfectly one, so that the world may know that thou has sent me and hast loved them even as thou hast loved me. Father, I desire that they also, whom thou hast given me, may be with me where I am, to behold my glory which thou hast given me in thy love for me before the foundation of the world. O righteous Father, the world has not known thee, but I have known thee; and these know that thou hast sent me. I made known to them thy name, and I will make it known, that the love with which thou hast loved me may be in them, and I in them." Amen.

Chapter 4

"One to Watch"

We spoke earlier of Matthew, Mark and Luke as a trinity of Gospels related to each other closely, perhaps as siblings, perhaps as first cousins. Of this trinity and in terms of our four angels, Mark is our "One to Watch." And this is so for two reasons. We "watch" Mark because his story of Jesus is the earliest of our New Testament Gospels. We "watch" Mark in his own right first, for we will see most of his Gospel appear in both Matthew and Luke, each written a generation later. And secondly, Mark is our "One to Watch" because the Gospel of Mark is the story of urgency and "watch" is Mark's own word. To this, we will return.

Because his is the earliest Gospel and the one on whom both Matthew and Luke are dependent, we are inclined to suggest that Mark ought to be in first place in the Scriptures. Mark is, however, in second place on purpose. Our faithful forebears of the second century were just as clever as we are. They, too, could tell that Matthew, Mark and Luke were a trinity of related Gospels. And they could tell that much of Matthew was very much like Mark. However, they drew the opposite conclusion from their observations that we draw. They noticed that there is a lot of stuff in Mark about the apostle Peter. They noticed that Mark had no story of Jesus' birth and no resurrection appearances. Instead of assuming that Mark preceded Matthew, they decided that Mark was a distillation or abbreviation of Matthew. They decided that this *Reader's Digest* version was not only later than Matthew but not nearly as useful as Matthew himself. And it became tradition that was taken for granted that the second Gospel was a shortened version of the first, cherished by a faithful community that looked back to the apostle Peter for teaching and spirituality. When the Gospels were lined up in the order of their usefulness and their importance, Mark got second place.

Somewhere around the time of the Reformation, our people began to look at the other side of the coin. "Maybe Mark is *not* an abbreviated version of Matthew at all," they said. "Maybe Matthew is a longer, more complete version of Mark." "In fact," they added, "Matthew and Luke both look like this. What if Mark was written a generation earlier than either of the other two?" And for more than the past 200 years, this has been the prevalent scholarly view. To this day, there are articulate and vociferous minority viewpoints. Some students of the New Testament will climb out on the limb that supports Luke as the earliest of this trinity of Gospels. Some students of the New Testament will claim that Matthew was written in Aramaic and was the first of the Gospels to be written, then later translated into the Greek in which we have the Gospel today. Sometimes the company on these limbs is very good indeed, but they are limbs nevertheless. For our purposes, we stand at the trunk of the tree with the majority and claim Mark as the earliest, the "One to Watch."

There is a book with which to watch the "One to Watch." This book is called *Gospel Parallels* and is edited by Burton Throckmorton, Jr. It is a synopsis of our first three Gospels, and it offers us the easiest and clearest way to see how Matthew, Mark and Luke relate to each other. These three Gospels lie next to each other on the pages of *Gospel Parallels*. And in this way, we can see both Mark within the stories of the other two as well as Matthew and Luke's fashioning of their own work.

We recall that each of the four Gospels has a two-part story of Jesus, a story of the ministry and a story of the passion. And we remember that the Gospel of John is the one in which these two sections are almost perfectly balanced in length. The first half of John is about the ministry; the second half of John is the story of the passion, wrapped around Jesus' "This is who I am . . . " teaching. If John is the most "balanced" of the Gospels in this manner, then Mark is the most "imbalanced."

Our second Gospel has often been described as "a passion narrative with an extended introduction." This is fair. For Mark, the events that lead to Jesus' death and crucifixtion influence the story of Jesus' ministry. We might even say that Mark tells the story backwards. That is, he cannot and will not begin even to tell his story of Jesus until the reader's attention is firmly focussed upon the cross. Further, Mark is not only our earliest Gospel; it is also our shortest Gospel. There are only sixteen chapters in the entire book, and Jesus' entry into Jerusalem begins with the first verse of Chapter 11. This means that nearly one-half of the book is about the passion, Jesus' "last days." A diagram of the second Gospel looks something like this:

Mark 1-16
The Passion of Jesus
through His Ministry

Mark's Gospel does not begin with the words "In the beginning . . . " or even a story of Jesus' birth, as do both Matthew and Luke. The first words of Mark are "The beginning of the gospel of Jesus Christ, the Son of God." (1:1) Immediately, the reader is plunged into the ministry of John the Baptizer. In the first thirteen verses of this first chapter, Mark's reader learns that John the Baptist foretold Jesus' coming and baptized Jesus in the Jordan. We are told that the Spirit descended upon Jesus, that there was a heavenly voice calling Jesus the "Beloved Son," that the Spirit drove Jesus into the wilderness where he was tempted by Satan and ministered to by angels. In Mark 1:14, Jesus' ministry begins with these words: "Now after John was arrested, Jesus came into Galilee, preaching the gospel of God and saying, 'The time is fulfilled, and the kingdom of God is at hand; repent and believe in the gospel,' " Once said, we plunge a second time into the events of Jesus' ministry. And there is an urgency and an immediacy to this ministry that we experience nowhere else.

Some of this urgency comes from Mark's style. The syntax of his narrative is clear and precise. While his story of Jesus is colorful and full of detail, he also tends to spit it out so that the very telling of it gives it speed. Indeed, the verb "to tell" is originally a counting verb, the one from which we get the term "bank teller." More than any of our other authors, Mark "tells" his version of Jesus' ministry and passion.

The urgency of Mark's story also has an immediacy to it. And the author intends that this "now-ness" be the tone of his Gospel. The word "immediately" in Greek is *euthus*. The adverb *euthus* only turns up in the Gospels; it never occurs in the Letters. And *euthus* does occur in all four Gospels. Luke uses *euthus* once in the third Gospel and once in Acts. Matthew uses the adverb seven times and on three occasions, *euthus* occurs in John. Mark uses *euthus* forty-two times in this, the smallest of our Gospels. This is remarkable. So, too, is the fact that he uses the adverb eleven times in the first chapter alone. "Immediately" begins to characterize Mark's story as soon as Jesus comes into Galilee, proclaiming the kingdom of God. Listen to the urgency in these first moments of Jesus' ministry:

> And passing along by the Sea of Galilee, he saw Simon and Andrew the brother of Simon casting a net in the sea; for they were fishermen. And Jesus said to them, "Follow me and I will make you become fishers of men." And *immediately* they left their nets and followed him. And going on a little farther, he saw James the son of Zebedee and John his brother, who were in their boat mending the nets. And *immediately* he called them; and they left their father Zebedee in the boat with the hired servants and followed him.
>
> And they went into Capernaum; and *immediately* on the sabbath he entered the synagogue and taught. And they were astonished at his teaching, for he taught them as one who had authority, and not as the scribes. And *immediately* there was in their synagogue a man with an unclean spirit; and he cried out, "What have you to do with us, Jesus of Nazareth? Have you come to destroy

us? I know who you are, the Holy One of God." But
Jesus rebuked him, saying, "Be silent, and come out of
him." And the unclean spirit, convulsing him and cry-
ing with a loud voice, came out of him. And they were
all amazed, so that they questioned among themselves,
saying, "What is this? A new teaching! With authority
he commands even the unclean spirits, and they obey
him." And *immediately* his fame spread everywhere
throughout all the surrounding region of Galilee. And
immediately he left the synagogue, and entered the
house of Simon and Andrew, with James and John."
(1:16-29)

This is Mark's heaviest concentration of "immediately." Mark's "immediatelys" continue to occur
throughout the second Gospel, so that we get the feel-
ing that we are racing toward the cross. Only in Chapter
13 does the reader get a rest. Jesus has taken Peter and
James and John and Andrew to the Mount of Olives
opposite the temple for last words of instruction. There
is no need for the adverb *euthus* in Mark 13, for this is
Jesus' teaching on the severity of the times to come.
"Take heed that no one leads you astray . . . " Jesus
says, "and when you hear of wars and rumors of wars,
do not be alarmed; this must take place, but the end is
not yet." (13:5-7)

Here in Chapter 13, Mark holds his language of immediacy to the side for a moment so that Jesus can tell
his disciples to "watch." It is as if all of the "immediatelys" so far have led to this very specific instruction.
Listen to the way this tone changes in Jesus' words:

Heaven and earth will pass away, but my words will
not pass away. But of that day or that hour no one
knows, not even the angels in heaven, nor the Son, but
only the Father. *Take heed*, *watch*; for you do not know
when the time will come. It is like a man going on a
journey, when he leaves home and puts his servants in

> charge, each with his work and commands the door-keeper to be on the *watch. Watch* therefore, for you do not know when the master of the house will come, in the evening, or at midnight, or at cock crow, or in the morning, lest he come suddenly and find you asleep. And what I say to you I say to all: *Watch*. (13:32-37)

Mark uses three different Greek verbs to make his point. His "take heed" in v. 33 can also be translated as "look," delivered in an insistent tone of voice. The "watch" that follows this "take heed" is an unusual verb. *Agrypneo* occurs nowhere else in Mark and rarely in the rest of the New Testament. It actually means "stay awake" or "be on the alert." It is precisely what the disciples do *not* do in the garden as Jesus prays before he is betrayed. The remaining three uses of "watch" are from the verb *gregoreo*, the most common Greek way to command alertness. Our name Gregory is a derivative of this Greek verb.

In every way that he can think of, Mark has recorded Jesus' words so that his disciples will be ready for that which is to come. They are to "watch." And once they have been so instructed, our author turns back to his narrative. Mark announces the Passover and the Feast of Unleavened Bread in 14:1, and our familiar "immediately" returns as Jesus begins to move through his "last days."

Mark's "immediately" disappears abruptly when Peter has denied Jesus, and the religious authorities have delivered Jesus into Pilot's hands. (15:1) Our author no longer has need of the adverb. The urgency has been conveyed and the immediacy has rushed us into Jesus' trial. A little breathlessly, we suddenly realize that our urgent journey has brought us to the foot of the cross.

We recognize this cross, for we also realize that we have journeyed in its shadow all along the way. As early as in the beginning of Chapter 3, we are told that in response to Jesus' Sabbath healing of the man with the withered hand, the Pharisees "immediately held counsel with the Herodians against Jesus, how to destroy him." (3:6) Midway in his ministry, Jesus goes home to Galilee to teach, and his own people take "offense" at him. (6:1-6)

On three occasions, Jesus predicts his crucifixion. The first of these occurs after the second miraculous feeding of a multitude. "Who do men say that I am?" he asks the disciples. "You are the Christ," Peter answers correctly. The author tells us that Jesus "charged them to tell no one about him. And [that] he began to teach them that the Son of man must suffer many things, and be rejected by the elders and the chief priests and the scribes, and be killed, and after three days rise again." (8:30-31) After the transfiguration, and while passing through Galilee, Jesus again says to his disciples, "The Son of man will be delivered into the hands of men and they will kill him; and when he is killed, after three days he will rise." (9:31) The third prediction comes as they near Jerusalem. Jesus says, "Behold, we are going up to Jerusalem; and the Son of man will be delivered to the chief priests and the scribes, and they will condemn him to death, and deliver him to the Gentiles; and they will mock him, and spit upon him and scourge him, and kill him; and after three days he will rise." (10:33-34)

Alongside the explicit predictions, there are also subtle references to the crucifixion. Jesus has triumphantly entered Jerusalem and is teaching in the temple. Mark tells us that a widow contributes two copper coins to the treasury. "Truly, I say to you," Jesus observes, "this poor widow has put in more than all who are contributing to the treasury. For they all contributed out of their abundance, but she out of her poverty has put in everything she had, her whole living." (12:43-44) So, too, Jesus contributes his "whole living."

At the same time that Mark casts the shadow of the cross over the whole Gospel, he tells this story so that his reader can see Jesus' ministry is one that gives life. This is a poignant contradiction; Jesus walks toward death as the blind can see, the dead come back to life, his followers experience life.

Mark builds this contradiction into the shape of his story of Jesus' ministry. We have seen the urgency and immediacy, and walked through some of the references to the crucifixion. These all occur within a framework that is divided into three sections. Our author himself thinks of this ministry in three parts, for each of these sections is preceded by spacing in the Greek text. Further, each of these sections closes with a spectacular story of healing, a story in which Jesus restores life. An outline of Jesus' ministry in Mark looks like this:

> *Jesus in the Wilderness*
>   1:14-5:43   Part I
>   Life Restored to Jairus' Daughter (5:1-43)
>   6:1-8:26   Part II
>   Sight Restored to the Blind Man (8:22-26)
>   8:27-10:52   Part III
>   Sight Restored to Bartimaeus (10:46-52)
> *Jesus' Entry into Jerusalem*

Mark's readers would not have missed the divisions between these sections as they read this story for themselves or aloud for others. And they would not have missed the significance of the life-giving story at the end of each one. Nor would they have missed the shadow of the cross or the urgency and immediacy with which Mark's entire story of Jesus' ministry is told.

When we put Mark's structure and the cross and the immediacy together, we find the author's intentions and the reason that Mark is the "One to Watch." When we put the structure and the cross and the immediacy of Jesus' ministry together, Mark urgently tells us that the cross means life. It is as if Mark says, "Here, look at this now and see this well: Though he walks toward crucifixion, Jesus brings life to the world." This is Mark's "gospel," the "good news" that he announces in the first words of his book.

This is not, however, all the news that there is in the second Gospel. We know of no word in Greek for "bad news," but there *is* some of this in Mark and this "bad news" is about discipleship. The beginning of this "bad news" is woven through the story of Jesus' ministry and comes to a climax in the passion.

Mark never lets his reader forget that Jesus' ministry has a contradiction at its heart, that Jesus walks toward death as he brings life into the world. We have seen Mark tell us of the opposition that Jesus' life-giving ministry calls forth, opposition from both the religious authorities and his own people. Mark also tells us that Jesus' life-giving ministry causes confusion, particularly from his own disciples.

There are three such occasions with Jesus and the disciples on the sea. Early in the ministry, a storm arises as Jesus and the disciples cross the sea. The disciples awaken Jesus in a panic. "Teacher, do you not care if

we perish?'' they frantically ask. Jesus calms the sea
and challenges their faith. Mark tells us that ''they were
filled with awe and said to one another, 'Who then is
this, that even wind and sea obey him?' '' (4:35-41)
Again on the sea after the feeding of the five thousand,
the disciples see Jesus walk upon the water. They cry
out in terror. Jesus reassures them, gets into the boat
and stills the wind that has blown against them. ''They
were utterly astounded,'' Mark explains, ''for they did
not understand about the loaves, but their hearts were
hardened.'' (6:45-52) On the third occasion, we can almost hear the frustration in Jesus' words:

> . . . Jesus said to them, ''Why do you discuss the
> fact that you have no bread? Do you not yet perceive or
> understand? Are your hearts hardened? Having eyes do
> you not see, and having ears do you not hear? And do
> you not remember? When I broke the five loaves for the
> five thousand, how many baskets full of broken pieces
> did you take up?'' They said to him, ''Twelve.'' ''And
> the seven for the four thousand, how many baskets full
> of broken peices did you take up?'' And they said to
> him, ''Seven.'' And he said to them, ''Do you not yet
> understand?'' (8:17-21)

On two other occasions in Jesus' ministry, Peter has
the privilege of expressing this confusion. Both of these
incidents occur just after Jesus has asked the disciples
''Who do men say that I am?'' Peter has given the cor-
rect answer; he has replied with ''You are the Christ.''
Jesus then predicts his passion for the first time and
Peter rebukes him. Surely, it is confusion that leads Peter to such foolishness. Jesus' response is severe. ''Get
behind me, Satan!'' Jesus says after he has rebuked Peter in return. ''For you are not on the side of God, but
of men.'' (8:27-33) The other occasion is not so harsh.
Six days and some teaching later, Jesus is transfigured

on the mountain. Elijah and Moses appear and talk with Jesus. Peter's confused and even more foolish response is to interrupt. "Master," he says to Jesus, "it is well that we are here; let us make three booths, one for you and one for Moses and one for Elijah." Mark explains that Peter "did not know what to say, for they were exceedingly afraid." (9:2-6)

The disciples' confusion reaches a climax in Mark's story of the passion. At the last, Jesus is abandoned by those who have followed him along the way. Of the twelve, Judas is the first to desert Jesus. In exchange for money, he offers to betray Jesus to the chief priests. At the Last Supper, Jesus tells them how this will be. "You will all fall away," he says. "For it is written, 'I will strike the shepherd, and the sheep will be scattered.' But after I am raised up, I will go before you to Galilee." Peter protests. "Even though they all fall away, I will not," he says. Jesus knows better, and says so. Mark tells us the end of the story: "But [Peter] said vehemently, 'If I must die with you, I will not deny you.' And they all said the same." (14:27-31)

Judas betrays Jesus in the garden. And as Jesus says the words, "But let the scriptures be fulfilled," Mark tells us that this is indeed the case. "And they all forsook him and fled," says Mark. (14:49-50)

No one but Peter returns. Peter follows at a distance as Jesus is led to the high priest. He warms himself at the fire in the courtyard and denies Jesus twice to a maid. "I do not know this man of whom you speak," he says to a bystander on the third occasion. The cock crows for a second time, and Peter weeps. (14:66-72) Jesus is alone.

A stranger from Cyrene carries Jesus' cross. An unnamed centurion recognizes him on the cross as "the Son of God." A stranger from Arimathea buries his body. Only the women who have followed him attend him at his death. Even those women who witness the empty tomb "went out and fled from the tomb; for trembling and astonishment had come upon them; and they said nothing to any one, for they were afraid." (16:8)

The "bad news" of Mark's Gospel is that under pressure and out of confusion, Jesus is abandoned by those whom he has chosen, those whom he has called, those who have accompanied him all along the way. And this is where our second Gospel ends. There are no resurrection appearances. We are not told of Jesus' reconciliation with the disciples. There is no event in which we learn that the women overcome their fear and do as they have been told. There is nothing to end our Gospel but talk of fear and flight.

Mark knows both urgency and immediacy in his own day, the day in which he writes our second Gospel. We cannot tell whether or not the soldiers of the Roman Empire are already at Jerusalem's gates. If not, they are certainly near. Mark's community faces the unimaginable crisis of Jerusalem's destruction. Under such pressure and in the face of such a crisis, Mark's community may legitimately ask, "Jesus, where are you when we need you?" and "How may we be faithful and know what to do next?"

Our second Gospel is Mark's answer to these questions. He reminds his community that as Jesus himself walked toward the crucifixion, he brought life into the world. He reminds them that Jesus' tomb is empty. He reminds them that the very worst that can happen to the faithful is fear and flight. "Watch," our author commands.

Mark does not reassure his community that times will be easy. If anything, he insists that they face the worst, the possibility of suffering and death. Neither, however, does Mark suggest or encourage despair. In Jesus' words, Mark holds out hope. There is implicit hope in his command to "watch," hope that those who watch will also see. And there is explicit hope in Jesus' promise in 13:11:

> "And when they bring you to trial and deliver you up, do not be anxious beforehand what you are to say; but say whatever is given to you in that hour, for it is not you who speak, but the Holy Spirit."

Mark holds out hope for those who would follow, for those who would be faithful. For this, he is our "One to Watch." Amen.

Chapter 5

"One to Keep Us Till the Day: Matthew the Teacher"

"One to watch, one to pray, two to keep me till the day"—this is our prayer. We ask the authors of our Gospels to be our guardians, to be our "angels." And through our prayer, we find this guardianship first in protection. So it is that we pray for Mark "to watch" and John "to pray."

We seek nurture as well as protection, and so we pray for two to keep us "till the day." Learning and healing are the ways in which Jesus makes the "good news" and the Kingdom of God known in our Gospels. How right it is that the ministries of the two to keep us "till the day" reflect Jesus' own ministry. And so it is that we may turn to Luke as "One to Heal" and to Matthew as "One to Teach."

Matthew's outstretched hand is the one to whom the church reached out first. We noted earlier that it is not by accident or coincidence that Matthew is our first Gospel. As soon as there *were* stories of Jesus, our people especially valued Matthew's carefully designed and carefully written account. In the light of the resurrection, our people asked some of the same questions we ask today, questions like: "How do we know that Jesus is Lord?" "Where in our Scripture does it explain how this is so?" "How are we to live faithful lives?" "What are we to do next?" Matthew, as do all our Gospels, has answers to these questions.

In Matthew's time, our people are still a Jewish people, concerned about living faithful Jewish lives
through their recognition of Jesus as Lord, as Messiah.
Matthew writes to such a community approximately a
decade prior to the turn of the first century. The hand
that Matthew offers his community is what we could
call a "kosher" one. He tells the story of Jesus, the
Messiah, within the context of faithful Jewish life.

In the years that follow, our people become less and
less Jewish and more and more Gentile in ethnic and
religious origin. In this time, Matthew is recognizably
the most "Jewish" of the Gospels, the most "kosher"
of Jewish-Christian writings. In this time, the hand that
Matthew holds out to the faithful becomes a bridge.
Our people are beginning to think of themselves as
"Christians," and Matthew's hand holds them firmly
to the earliest days, to their Jewish tradition, their Jewish roots. When our people began to think of themselves as "Christians" and as "the church," we turned to
Matthew as the "one to teach."

It is also true that Matthew wrote his story of Jesus
for "the church" and the church could see this from the
start. Our word for "church" comes from the Greek
word *ekklesia* and means "those who are called out."
"those who are called forth." In English, we also get
terms like "ecclesiastical" and "ecclesiology" from the
same word.

The word itself is created by adding the proposition
ek to the front of the verb *kaleo*. And as is so often the
case, our English translation doesn't quite say what the
Greek intends. To talk of the *ekklesia* is to talk about
God and the People of God and something of their

relationship all in the same breath. The name *ekklesia* actually describes a divine process. The *ekklesia* is the result of God's call, God's desire for a people, God's desire to be in relationship with this people. It is a privilege and something of a miracle to be part of an *ekklesia*, and God's people are responsible for thanksgiving and praise in return. In part, this is Matthew's message as our "angel," the one to whom we turn as "the one to teach." *Ekklesia* is Matthew's word and he is the only author of our four Gospels to use the term. Matthew understands the faithful as "the church" and writes for "the church." "Those who were called out" have always known that this is so.

Matthew uses *ekklesia* twice. The first occasion is our author's version of the Markan story we have seen before. Jesus asks the disciples, "Who do men say that the Son of man is?" When they have answered, he asks again, "But who do you say that I am?" As in Mark, Peter has the right answer. At the same time, it is a slightly different answer. He says, "You are the Christ, the Son of the living God." In Matthew's story, Jesus replies:

> "Blessed are you, Simon Bar-Jona. For flesh and blood has not revealed this to you, but my Father who is in heaven. And I tell you, you are Peter, and on this rock I will build my *ekklesia*, and the gates of Hades shall not prevail against it. I will give you the keys of the kingdom of heaven, and whatever you bind on earth shall be bound in heaven, and whatever you loose on earth shall be loosed in heaven." (Matthew 16:13-19, my translation)

Matthew tells us that Jesus renames Peter at the same time that he commissions him as the leader of his "church." At the onset of Jesus' words, Peter's name is Simon, son of Jonas. But Simon is now to be called *Petros*, "the rock." On "this *petros*," Jesus will build his "church." With Peter as the "rock," the foundation of the *ekklesia* will be so strong that the strength of evil and death will not overcome it. Jesus' words are a promise that looks beyond Peter's denial and through the resurrection to the life of the faithful in community.

Following this promise, Matthew lays out a number of regulations for the life of this faithful community. And this is where his second use of *ekklesia* occurs:

> "If your brother sins against you, go and tell him his fault, between you and him alone. If he listens to you, you have gained your brother. But if he does not listen, take one or two others along with you, that every word may be confirmed by the evidence of two or three witnesses. If he refuses to listen to them, tell it to the *ekklesia*; and if he refuses to listen even to the *ekklesia*, let him be to you as a Gentile and a tax collector. Truly, I say to you, whatever you bind on earth shall be bound in heaven, and whatever you loose on earth shall be loosed in heaven. Again I say to you, if two of you agree on earth about anything they ask, it will be done for them by my Father in heaven. For where two or three are gathered in my name, there am I in the midst of them." (Matthew 18:15-20)

Jesus' words in Matthew are very clear about the way in which the faithful are to settle their differences. In this process, the privacy of the dispute is respected in the first order. The difference may be taken into an intimate gathering of witnesses in the second order. The final step is to enter the dispute into the life of the community of the faithful, the "church," those whom God has called out. And the community of the faithful offers a judgment that is binding. If the other in the dispute does not abide by the community's decision, he or she is to be dismissed and ignored. They are to be treated as a "Gentile and a tax collector." In both Jesus' and Matthew's day, Gentiles and tax collectors must live their lives outside of the life of the faithful Jewish community.

In both of these passages, Jesus says, "Whatever you bind on earth shall be bound in heaven, and whatever you loose on earth shall be loosed in heaven." And in both of these passages, the *ekklesia* is foreseen as "the body of Christ." This is Matthew's way of telling us that in his ministry, Jesus commissioned the community of the faithful to represent himself and God on earth. Whatever the *ekklesia* does on earth, God in heaven will honor, God will "bind and loose."

In Jesus' last words of the Gospel, we can hear echoes of Matthew's teaching on the *ekklesia*. In the light of the resurrection, Jesus meets the eleven disciples in Galilee and commissions them once and for all with the following:

> "All authority in heaven and on earth has been given to me. Go therefore and make disciples of all nations, baptizing them in the name of the Father and of the Son and of the Holy Spirit, teaching them to observe all that I have commanded you; and lo, I am with you always, to the close of the age." (Matthew 28:18-20)

According to Matthew, the church will be strong enough to withstand evil and just enough to arbitrate human affairs. With all of the authority "in heaven and on earth," Jesus commissions the *ekklesia* to baptize and to teach until the end of time as time is known upon earth. And our first Gospel closes with Jesus' promise to be with the *ekklesia* for all this time, "to the

close of the age.'' Our people took this promise
and this responsibility seriously. The *ekklesia* took
Matthew's outstretched hand when she needed regulations and structure and the promise of the presence of
the risen Lord. The ''church'' took Matthew's outstretched hand when she needed to hold fast to her tradition and her heritage as she walked forward to teach
and to learn the faith.

We have already spoken of the fact that Matthew
contains much of the Gospel of Mark. To Mark's story,
the author of our first Gospel adds a collection of sayings and stories of Jesus that we call ''Q'', as abbreviation for *quelle*, the German word for ''source.'' We
think of these sayings and stories as a collection and as
a ''source'' because we can see them in both Matthew
and Luke. Here again, *Gospel Parallels* is our helpmeet
and our guide. When Matthew and Luke lie beside each
other on the page, we are able to see their similarities
and differences. ''The Lord's Prayer'' is a good example of ''Q'' material. This prayer is so familiar to
us that it is almost startling when we discover that
Matthew and Luke's versions are not exactly the same.
And we are enriched precisely because they are different; we have Jesus' teaching, and then the emphases
and concerns of each author, of each ''angel.'' We are
able to see what Matthew would have us learn, what
Luke would have us understand.

In addition to Mark and ''Q'', Matthew has his own
material as well. We have already looked at his teaching
on the *ekklesia*. And we have mentioned his ''Great
Commission,'' the consummation of Jesus' teaching
upon earth. This is the only place in the Gospels where
the names of the Trinity appear in the church's for-

mula. And this is also the only place in the Gospels where baptism is mentioned with all three of God's names—the Father, the Son and the Holy Spirit. We hold Matthew's hand tightly in Jesus' words of commission. For throughout the church's many generations, these have been the words that weave baptism, learning and discipleship into a unique, yet ever-changing tapestry of Christian mission.

Matthew's beginning is as distinctive as his close. This is "the book of the genealogy of Jesus Christ, the son of David, the son of Abraham," he tells us. And he immediately launches into a long list of names—three sets of fourteen generations. Our "angel's" message would be very clear to a Jewish reader, for this is Jesus' family history and pedigree in the history of Judaism all tightly packed into seventeen verses. For a faithful Jewish man of the first century, a genealogy was absolutely essential. It was his identification, like a birth certificate, a driver's license and a Social Security card. It was his certification of religious membership, like a baptismal certificate or a parish letter. It was a set of generational credentials, like the births and marriages listed in the family Bible as well as the diplomas and portraits hung on the family walls. Genealogies were carefully remembered and carefully recorded and then stored in the Jerusalem temple for safe-keeping.

Matthew's readers would have noticed three things about this list of names. The first is that Jesus is called "Christ" twice, once at the beginning of the list and then again at its end. There is no mistaking Matthew's intention. He is making sure that his readers know that Jesus is the one "anointed" by God, the Messiah for whom the people have prayed throughout all generations.

Secondly, Matthew's Jewish readers would have noticed that this genealogy begins in the distant past and comes forward to the birth of Jesus. A family history may be traced in either direction. Our "angel" chooses to begin with Abraham, the one to whom God promised generations as numerous as the grains of sand and the heavenly stars. By tracing Jesus' family history from Abraham forward, Matthew says to his readers, "*Here* are the promised generations, as well as the Christ."

And finally, Jewish readers would be startled by the references to five women in this long list of "fathers." Matthew seems to have placed these references to women carefully in his list. Three of these women are named before "David the king"—Judah's wife Tamar; Rahab, the mother of Boaz; Boaz' wife Ruth. Matthew tells us that Solomon is the son of David and "the wife of Uriah," a woman whose name is surely intentionally omitted. Scandal has always accompanied David and Bathsheba. Matthew is no exception and treats David's fathering of Solomon by another man's wife as an unfortunate piece of history. From the generation of Solomon *forward* only fathers are named. Mary is suddenly mentioned in 1:16, and the effect is as if a spotlight shines on the list's last words: " . . . and Jacob the father of Joseph, the husband of Mary, of whom Jesus was born, who is called the Christ."

We have generations and generations of Sunday School pageants in our treasure of Christian traditions, and we forget that Matthew and Luke have very different stories of Jesus' birth. Once he has listed Jesus' family tree, our author of the first Gospel begins with "Now the birth of Jesus Christ took place in this way."

Matthew tells this story from a masculine point of view. The narrative is primarily concerned with Joseph's perspective and the principal characters are all men—Joseph, the boy-child, the magi, Herod, the chief priests and scribes. We will see how feminine Luke's version of this story is, and marvel at the balance of this, our good fortune in Scripture.

Matthew shows us Joseph's legitimate and poignant difficulty; his betrothed is pregnant before their marriage. Joseph is "a just man and unwilling to put her to shame, resolved to divorce her quietly." (1:19) And with this, Joseph's dreams begin. Through the events surrounding Jesus' birth, Joseph is guided by an "angel of the Lord" who comes to him in dreams. The angel explains Mary's conception to Joseph in 1:20, he is told to flee to Egypt in 2:13. Instructions for the family's return to Judea come to Joseph in a dream in 2:19. Finally, he is warned of the reign of Herod's son and withdraws with his family to Galilee. (2:22) In Matthew's story, God is in charge and beside Joseph all along the way. And it's a good thing, for the way is hard.

The moment that the child is born, magi from the East turn up on King Herod's doorsteps. They have read the heavens and have journeyed to Jerusalem. All that they know is that one has been born "king of the Jews," and his star has led them this far along their way. They ask Herod for directions. Herod assembles the chief priests and scribes and asks them to search the Scriptures to see where the Messiah, the Christ is to be born. The religious officials find the answer to Herod's question in the words of the prophet Micah. Herod sends the magi to Bethlehem with the added request of a report. The journey and homage of the magi result in the flight for which Joseph needs dream directions.

From the words of his introduction, the genealogy, and his story of Jesus' birth, Matthew tells us a story about Judaism, her traditions and her expectations and her fears. In this story, God answers the prayers of the People of God. And our author never loses an opportunity to tell his readers just exactly how this is so. Jesus is the answer to these prayers. Jesus' teaching and his interpretation of the Law and the prophets *fulfill* the Scriptures, Matthew tells us time and time again.

"This was to fulfill what the Lord had spoken . . . " is already Matthew's refrain in the story of Jesus' birth. It will become our clue that our "angel" is about to quote the Scriptures. It will also become one of the ways we can see Matthew and his community understand God's saving act of the life, death and resurrection of Jesus.

Sometimes, it is easy to see how Matthew makes the connection between an event in Jesus' story and the Scriptures. The angel's words to Joseph about Mary's conception are a good example:

> All this took place to fulfill what the Lord had spoken by the prophet: "Behold, a virgin shall conceive and bear a son, and his name shall be called Emmanuel" (which means God with us). (1:22-23)

Another place we can see Matthew make such a connection is in his account of Judas' death. It is from Matthew alone that we learn Judas went to the chief priests and elders to confess his sin of betrayal, how he leaves the money in the temple and hangs himself. Matthew explains that because of this event, the field is called the Field of Blood, and summarizes with the following:

> Then was fulfilled what was spoken by the prophet
> Jeremiah, saying, "And they took the thirty pieces of
> silver, the price of him on whom a price had been set by
> some of the sons of Israel, and they gave them for the
> potter's field, as the Lord directed me. (27:9-10)

Sometimes Matthew sees a connection that is not so
clear to those of us who read him ninety-nine generations later. This is the case in his story of Herod's murder of the children in Bethlehem and the surrounding
region. Our author says:

> Then was fulfilled what was spoken by the prophet
> Jeremiah: "A voice was heard in Ramah, wailing and
> loud lamentation, Rachel weeping for her children; she
> refused to be consoled, because they were no more."
> (2:17-18)

Whatever we may think about the appropriateness of
the connections that Matthew has made, we can see his
consistency. "Jesus fulfills the Scriptures," he insists.
We can practically hear the pages of his Bible rustle
when he points to passage after passage as he tells the
story of Jesus. This is one of the places in which he is
most clearly the "One to Teach." We are fortunate, for
we get a very good view of a first century rabbi, weav-
ing his Holy Scriptures with daily life in search of understanding. Then we can also see that his instruction
goes in two directions, that he teaches all of Judaism
something new about how God acts, how God is
known. First and foremost, he teaches his own community, showing them how it is that the events of Jesus'
life, death, and resurrection fulfill God's promises as
these promises are recorded in the Scriptures. "This *is*
the Messiah;" he says to his own people, "this *is* the

way it was always supposed to be.'' At the same time, he teaches those who do not yet believe. Matthew is also proving his scriptural points to the competition—other faithful Jews who do *not* believe that Jesus is the Messiah, the Anointed One promised by God.

Matthew's use of Holy Scripture is not the only way we can see him as a teacher. Indeed, the very structure of the first Gospel is designed by our ''angel'' to teach and to instruct others to teach as well. A picture of Matthew's shape looks like this:

Introduction Birth	Book I 3:1-7:29	Book II 8:1-11:1	Book III 11:2-13:52	Book IV 13:53-19:2	Book V 19:3-25:46	Conclusion Passion

From the structure of the Gospel, we can immediately understand the church's early and profound love of the book. In form as well as content, everything we could want in a Gospel is here. There is a birth story and there are stories about the resurrection—a proper beginning and a proper end. And then, Jesus' ministry is carefully laid out in an orderly fashion. To a Gentile reader, Matthew's design of the story of Jesus is useful and easy to comprehend. To a Jewish reader, Matthew's design is recognizable. The five books in Matthew that tell the story of Jesus' ministry can be compared to the first five books of the Hebrew Scriptures, the Torah or ''the Law.'' We think of these books as Genesis, Exodus, Leviticus, Numbers and Deuteronqmy. But in their Hebrew originals and even the Greek translation of the Old Testament, these five books are called Moses I, Moses II, Moses III, Moses IV and Moses V. No Jewish reader would have missed this similarity, and would have seen Matthew's five sections of the ministry as Jesus I, II, III, IV and V.

In his book *Matthew, the Teacher's Gospel*, Paul Minear describes the shape of the first Gospel with the following titles and themes:

> "The Origins of Jesus" (1:1-2:23)
>> "Beginnings in the Work of Salvation" (3:1-7:29)
>> "The Physician and the Crowds" (8:1-11:1)
>> "The Mysterious Presence of the Kingdom" (11:2-13:52)
>> "The Care of the Crowds" (13:53-19:2)
>> "Preparation for the Passion" (19:3-25:46)
> "Covenant and Mandate" (26:1-28:20)

Both of these diagrams illustrate Matthew's emphasis on Jesus' ministry. In Mark, we saw how the passion effected Mark's version of Jesus' ministry. And we saw how the Gospel of John is evenly divided between the story of the ministry and the story of the passion. Once we look at the shape of Matthew, we are a little startled to see how much more attention our author gives to the ministry than to the passion. Indeed, the birth narrative serves as an introduction to this story and the passion and resurrection appearances serve as its conclusion.

Finally, each one of these five books has a teaching "manual," a set of instructions as its conclusion:

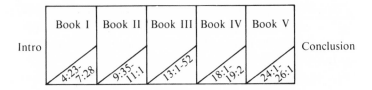

We are once again indebted to Minear for the titles of these collections of instructions; they are related, of course, to the content of each book. Each of these "manuals" ends with the expression "and when Jesus finished . . . " And this is Matthew's signal to his reader that this particular set of instructions has come to a close. When we arrive at the last of these sayings, we realize that both the teaching and Jesus' ministry are over:

> When Jesus had finished all these sayings, he said to his disciples, "You know that after two days the Passover is coming, and the son of man will be delivered up to be crucified." (26:1)

We have said before that in the Greek language, the arrangement of the material, even the arrangement of the words themselves is significant. The shape of each Gospel matters to each of our "angels," and we have looked carefully at their structures to see what each author would like for us to see and hear. There is a heart to Matthew's five books about Jesus' ministry. Our author, the "One to Teach," would not want us to miss this heart that lies at the center of his Gospel, for it offers something of his human heart to his readers as well.

The heart of Matthew's Gospel is, of course, at its

center—in Book III, "The Mysterious Presence of the Kingdom." This is the shortest, as well as the center of the five books. Perhaps we may also say that the teaching in this book is the most problematic as well. Jesus addresses issues of the distinction between good and evil, how some can "hear" and "see" truth and some cannot, and the mysteriousness of God's Kingdom. We may say that the teaching is problematic because the issues are not limited to Jesus' or Matthew's time. These are issues that have faced the faithful for all of their ninety-nine generations; they are issues that are our own today.

Our "angel" tells us that when Jesus finishes his teaching, he asks his disciples, "Have you understood all this?" They answer in the affirmative. Then he says to them, "Therefore every scribe who has been trained for the kingdom of heaven is like a householder who brings out of his treasure what is new and what is old." (13:51-52)

Jesus' words are unique to the first Gospel; they occur nowhere else. They are uniquely Matthean as well. The shape and the content of Matthew's Gospel suggest that the author himself is a scribe like the one that Jesus names. The scribes of the first century were all teachers. The "training" of the scribe that is mentioned is the Greek verb *matheteuo*—"to teach," "to learn." And this is the same word from which we get Matthew's name. Finally, our "angel" does what Jesus describes. As the teacher of Judaism and the teacher for Judaism, Matthew's Gospel tells a story that is both new and old. Matthew's story of Jesus' fulfillment of God's promises *is* written "like a householder who brings out of his treasure what is new and what is old." In this heart of the first Gospel, Matthew opens his own heart to his reader. It is a radiant heart and gleams like a fine gem in clear light.

When the dust of the first seige of Jerusalem had settled in 70 A.D., the religious world had to reorganize, reconstruct and rebuild itself. This was true for the Jews who believed Jesus to be the Messiah. This was also true for the Jews who believed that the Messiah was yet to come. We think that both of these groups of our faithful forebears gathered in southern Syria and northern Judea in order to sort themselves out. We know that around 90 A.D., the remnants of pharisaic Judaism gathered in Jamnia to decide upon the content and order of their Holy Scriptures and to discuss the future of worship in the synagogues. We think Matthew is their Christian-Jewish colleague and competition, teaching those who are to carry the "good news" of the one who fulfills the Law and the prophets.

Our "angel" insists that those who confess Jesus as Messiah must honor the tradition and "keep the faith." His Gospel was first in the hearts of our forebears who fashioned the Christian church; his Gospel is first in our Holy Scriptures for precisely this truth. When we reach out across ninety-nine generations to hold the hand that Matthew offers, we, too, receive his mandate to honor the tradition and "keep the faith." It is the right mandate as well as a radiant heart. For if we are to be the *ekklesia*, those whom God calls out, we must be trained like the scribe that was trained for the kingdom of heaven—the one who is "like a householder who brings out of his treasure what is new and what is old." The hand offered by the "One to Teach" is a wise hand to hold, indeed. Amen.

Chapter 6

"One to Keep Us Till the Day:
Luke the Healer"

When we turn to our guardian angels, we have John and Mark for protection, Matthew and Luke for nurture. And here, we move from Matthew's wise hands of learning to Luke's healing embrace. Luke is the last of our four "angels."

We come to Luke last because his Gospel is in the least important place; he has the third position out of four. We have learned that order and arrangement matter in Greek, that the beginnings and ends and centers of words or chapters or even stories about Jesus are significant and worthy of note. Matthew, we have said, is in first place on purpose. John is fourth of four because he came into the New Testament last. For something in the center to be important in Greek, there must be an uneven number. This is, for example, why we could see the significance of the third of the five books of Jesus' ministry in Matthew. Our Gospels are an even number, not an uneven one. Mark and Luke are the Gospels that are betwixt and between—important enough to become Holy Scripture, but not worthy of first or last place.

Before Irenaeus successfully argued for the inclusion of the Gospel of John, Luke was third. What we call the "New Testament," Irenaeus called the "Christian Writings." And from *Against Heresies,* we assume that

Irenaeus knew these Christian Writings in the following order: Matthew, Mark, Luke, Acts, Romans, 1 Corinthians, 2 Corinthians and so forth through Paul's letters. The shape of the Christian Writings changes when Irenaeus wins his arguement for the Gospel of John and the fourth Gospel slides into place.

Did Irenaeus have any idea how successfully he made his case? Did he know within his lifetime that his argument "worked?" We doubt it. Did Irenaeus have any idea that the Gospel of Luke and the Acts of the Apostles were written by the same author? We doubt it. We know that he does not ask the same questions about authorship that we do. And we *do* know that he calls all the Gospels and Acts "writings of the apostles," and trusts and values them as truthful bearers of the tradition. Did Irenaeus notice that the Gospel of John was put in the middle of Luke and Acts? We doubt it. Would Irenaeus care that he is responsible for interrupting the only two-volume work in the New Testament? We will never know. But he is.

From Irenaeus' day to this very day, faithful Christian communities have been unable to read the two-volume book the way that Luke, its author, would have us read it. Poor Luke. Before we can benefit from his healing embrace, we take *his* hand for consolation. And we reassure him that we will be sure to read these books together so that we can get his "message" straight.

This is not entirely Irenaeus' fault. Indeed, sometimes I think we are lucky that we have the Gospel of Luke in the New Testament canon at all. Much of the blame is to be laid at the feet of Marcion, an early church theologian who loved the Gospel of Luke too early, too well, and for several of the wrong reasons.

Marcion was excommunicated by the church in 144 A.D. As a churchman and a theologian and an interpreter of Scripture and tradition, he was wildly successful in his short-lived career. He rejected the Old Testament entirely, stating in no uncertain terms that he would have nothing to do with such a God of wrath. He preferred a Christ that was more divine than human, a Jesus who only "seemed" to be human. He limited the Christian Writings that his followers could read to an abbreviated version of the Gospel of Luke and a very carefully edited version of the Apostle Paul's letters. He insisted that this stuff—and this alone—was the "Holy Scripture" for the church. The Marcionite version of Luke and Paul's letters became the first "canon" of the New Testament, the first set of Christian Scriptures.

The church arose in rebellion. In our day, Verna Dozier says this about a Marcionite point of view:

> "If you think the God of the Old Testament is a God of wrath, then you don't know the prophets Isaiah and Jeremiah. If you think the God of the New Testament is a God of sweetness and light, then you don't know Jesus of Nazareth."

This is a good contemporary description of the position that the church took in the middle of the second century. As God's holy people, our Scriptures had always been the Scriptures of the Old Testament. "The Hebrew Scriptures are here to stay," our forebears insisted. "Furthermore, there is more to the story of Jesus than Marcion is willing to tell. The Old Testament and the unexpurgated version of the Gospel of Luke remain; Marcion goes." In reaction to Marcion's mean-spirited limitation of Holy Scripture and the person of

Jesus, our forbears begin to think seriously about the relationship of Jesus' life and work to God's promises in the Old Testament. In reaction to Marcion, our forebears begin to discuss what should and should not be included in collections of "Christian Writings." Ironically, Marcion's gift to the church is that he set the formation of Christian canon into process. Fortunately, the church did not throw the baby out with the bathwater. The Gospel of Luke stayed in third place; John became the fourth Gospel; Acts has remained forever between the Gospels and the Letters as the odd book out.

This means, of course, that when we reach out for Luke's healing embrace, the first thing our angel tells us is that "The Gospel of Luke" is not really a Gospel at all. It is, rather, Part I of a two-volume book. The Gospel is the story of Jesus' life and work, his sending out of the faithful and his crucifixion and resurrection. Acts is the story of the church's life and work, the sending out of the faithful and the advance of the "good news" throughout the world. In both Part I and Part II, the principal character is God in the person of the Holy Spirit. Luke-Acts is a theology, a two-volume book about God and creation—about who God is and how God is known.

Once we get Luke and Acts together, there are two ways to see this quickly. If we skim over the first chapters of the Gospel, we begin to notice how often the Holy Spirit is mentioned. Gabriel promises Zechariah that John will be "filled with the Holy Spirit." (Luke 1:15) Upon Mary's visit, Elizabeth is filled with the Holy Spirit in 1:41, Zechariah in 1:67. The Spirit comes to Simeon when Jesus is presented in the temple. (Luke

2:27) John the Baptist proclaims that Jesus "will baptize you with the Holy Spirit and with fire;" the Spirit descends upon Jesus in the form of a dove in his own baptism. (Luke 3:16,22) "Full of the Holy Spirit," Jesus is led "by the Spirit into the wilderness;" Jesus returns from the wilderness "in the power of the Spirit." (Luke 4:1,14) And what the Spirit begins in the Gospel, the Spirit continues in the book of Acts. The Holy Spirit is poured out upon the Jews in Jerusalem in Chapter 2, upon the Gentiles with Cornelius and his household in Chapter 10. And Paul's very last words in Acts invoke the Holy Spirit. (Acts 28:25)

The other way to see that Luke-Acts is a theology, and that these two books belong together is to look carefully at their introductions. In Chapter 1, we said that our author of the third Gospel knows and says that he is writing literature. There, we emphasized the fact that Luke calls his two-volume work an "orderly account." Here is this incredibly long introductory sentence again:

> Inasmuch as many have undertaken to compile a narrative of the things which have been accomplished among us, just as they were handed down to us by those who from the beginning were eyewitnesses and ministers of the word, it seemed good to me also, having followed all things from above accurately, to write an orderly account for you, most excellent Theophilos, that you may know the certain truth concerning the things of which you have been informed. (Luke 1:1-4, my translation)

And here is the way Part II begins:

> In the first book, O Theophilos, I have dealt with all that Jesus began to do and teach, until the day when he was taken up, after he had given commandment through the Holy Spirit to the apostles whom he had chosen . . . (Acts 1:1-2)

Both books are addressed to someone named *Theophilos*, which means "friend of God" or "lover of God" in Greek. The introductions are personal; the author refers to himself as "I" and Theophilos as "you" in the familiar second person. The introduction to Acts sounds as if the author is picking up where he left something off and this is precisely what has happened. For publishing reasons, our author must stop his story with Jesus' resurrection appearances and begin a new book. In the first century, books were published most often on papyrus rolls of 25-35 feet long. The Gospel of Luke would take one entire roll and Acts would take another. Two scrolls are necessary for our angel to tell his story about God and God's creation, God's incarnation in Jesus of Nazareth and God's forever-power in the Holy Spirit. Two scrolls are necessary for Luke to stretch out his hand and offer a healing embrace.

Our tradition has always been that the author of the third Gospel and Acts is "Luke, the beloved physician." This title comes, however, from a letter written by one of Paul's disciples to the Colossians. (Col. 4:14) The tradition is appropriate, and though we can never prove it—it may even be true. As we do, our forebears could see that the third Gospel has more emphasis upon Jesus' ministry of healing than Matthew, Mark or John. Luke's healing stories stand out, then and now. In our time, however, we can see even more evidence for the tradition. Luke uniquely distinguishes among "caring," "curing," and "healing" with his Greek vocabulary. Much of this language occurs nowhere else in the New Testament, but does have parallels in the medical journals and records of the first century.

For Luke, the life and work of Jesus of Nazareth is

healing for the world. For Luke, the power of God's Holy Spirit and the incarnation of God in Jesus is healing for the world. For Luke, the power of evil in the world is overcome by the power of God's Spirit in the person of Jesus and in the life and work of the faithful. This is true, our angel says, before and after the resurrection. This is true, Luke claims, from the moment of Gabriel's good news for Zechariah until this very day. The healing embrace that our angel of Luke-Acts offers describes a creation that is healed when God and creation love each other in return.

Earlier, we watched Matthew show his community how God's promises in the Old Testament had come true and, in particular, how Jesus fulfills God's promise to send a Messiah—the Christ, the "Anointed One." Our author of Luke-Acts shares this belief in God's promises come true with Matthew. It is not, however, Luke's style to quote the Old Testament with the introductory "thus was fulfilled . . . " As Luke narrates his two-volume work, more often than not his characters will quote the Scriptures for him. As narrator of the first Gospel, we have seen Matthew reserve this privilege for himself. In addition, Luke's narrative is written in the style and language of the Old Testament as it is heard and read in the Greek translation. Our angel tells his story so that it will sound like Scripture and so that his readers will hear their own Scriptures in its words. For example, when Gabriel tells Mary of Elizabeth's conception, he says, "For with God nothing will be impossible." Mary's well-known reply is "Behold, I am the handmaid of the Lord; let it be to me according to your word." (Luke 1:37-38) Luke's readers would instantly recognize the "with God nothing is impossible" as God's words from the Scriptures. And they would remember the stories of other barren women—Rachel, Leah, Sarah. They would remember Sarah's laughter at the news of God's promise to Abraham; they would remember God's rebuke, "Is anything too hard for the Lord?" (Gen. 18:14) From the way that Luke weaves the words and phrases of the Scriptures with the telling of the story itself, his readers would hear the words that are *not* there, the point that Luke wants to make: "Mary did not laugh."

Not only is Luke's style different than Matthew's; he also has entirely different passages from the Old Testament in mind. God's promise to Moses on the deliverance side of the Red Sea lies at the heart of Luke's healing embrace: "I am the Lord, your healer." (Ex. 15:26)

Luke can see God the healer in his Scriptures, and in particular in the book of the prophet Isaiah. Luke knows that before Isaiah can bring God's healing power to the Chosen People, Isaiah must first bring God's anger:

> Go and say to this people, "Hear and hear, but do not understand; see and see, but do not perceive." Make the heart of this people fat and their ears heavy, and shut their eyes, lest they see with their eyes, and hear with their ears, and understand with their hearts, and turn and be healed." (Is. 6:9-10)

But Luke also knows that God turns and reverses these harsh words, that the word of the Lord to Second Isaiah is the word of forgiveness and promise:

> But now says the Lord, he who created you, O Jacob, he who formed you, O Israel: "Fear not, for I have redeemed you; I have called you by name, you are mine . . . Fear not, for I am with you; I will bring your

> offspring from the east, and from the west I will gather
> you; I will say to the north, Give up, and to the south,
> Do not withhold; bring my sons from afar and my
> daughters from the end of the earth, everyone who is
> called by my name, whom I created for my glory, whom
> I formed and made. Bring forth the people who are
> blind, yet have eyes, who are deaf, yet have ears!" (Is.
> 43:1-8)

And Luke knows that God's forgiveness and restoration carry a mandate, that as God heals the Chosen People, so too the People of God are to heal God's creation:

> The Spirit of the Lord God is upon me, because the
> Lord has anointed me to bring good tidings to the af-
> flicted; he has sent me to bind up the broken hearted, to
> proclaim liberty to the captives, and the opening of the
> prison to those who are bound; to proclaim the year of
> the Lord's favor. (Is. 61:1-2)

As surely as Luke recognizes God as the healer in Holy Scripture, Luke recognizes God the healer in his own time and his own community. The "narratives" about Jesus with which he is acquainted do not tell the story of Jesus the way that Luke knows it to be true. And so it is that when our author fashions his "orderly account," these very words from Isaiah inaugurate Jesus' ministry. For Luke, Jesus' life and work really begin in the wilderness, so he includes Jesus' baptism with the ministry of John the Baptist in Chapter 3, and inserts his own genealogy between the events. Even the Greek text of the third Gospel emphasizes the author's point. There is a break between the third and fourth chapters, a signal from the manuscript itself that a new section of the story has begun.

Jesus returns from the wilderness in the power of the

Spirit into Galilee. He goes home to worship, is given the book of the prophet Isaiah to read in the synagogue on the sabbath day. He reads from Isaiah 61, beginning with "The Spirit of the Lord is upon me . . . " He closes the book, returns it "to the attendant" and sits down. Luke tells us that "the eyes of all in the synagogue were fixed on him." Jesus then says, "Today this scripture has been fulfilled in your hearing." (Luke 4:16-21)

"Here is the truth, the *asphaleia*, about what you have heard," our angel says in the introduction to the Gospel. "God's power and presence in the world as the Holy Spirit and the life, death and resurrection of Jesus of Nazareth are God's promise come true. 'I am your healer,' the Lord our God says, and this is so to this very day."

"And here is what you must do," he says to the faithful in Part II of his story. "Devote yourselves to the apostles' teaching, to fellowship, to the breaking of bread and to the prayers." (Acts 2:42) Luke knows that this is all that the faithful must do. In the Gospel this is actually all that the faithful must do. In the Gospel this is actually all that Jesus does: he devotes himself to his religious tradition of the temple and the synagogue; he participates in table-fellowship with everyone from his own disciples to tax collectors, women and Pharisees; he often withdraws from his daily life of teaching and healing for sustinence through prayer. Because Jesus does this in the power of the Holy Spirit, it works. The blind can see, the lame are healed, those captive by possession are set free. The honesty of Jesus' faith is recognizable by those who follow him. And the same is true, our angel says, for those whom Jesus commissions—the twelve and then the seventy in Chapters 9 and 10 of the Gospel. Indeed, the same is true for those who call upon Jesus' name in Acts, the faithful who walk for God in creation in the light of the resurrection. Peter says to Aeneas, bedridden and paralyzed for eight years, "Jesus Christ heals you." (Acts 9:34)

Luke knows that this healing love is different than what happens when a disease or an infirmity is "cured." The healing of creation that Luke describes in the third Gospel and Acts is the healing of restoration, the reversal of the process of disintegration, the reunification of God and God's own creation in love. Wholeness is the result of healing.

Luke must find a way to tell his reader that "curing" and "healing" are not the same thing. He does this by adding the verb *iaomai* to his story of Jesus and his story of the faithful. There are twenty-one occurrences of *iaomai* in the New Testament and fifteen of them belong to our author. He reserves them for whole-making "healing" and uses the far more common *therapeuo* for "curing." "Curing" is what actually happens when a blind person can see or a lame person can walk.

It is interesting that we have inherited both of these Greek verbs in our own English vocabulary. The side-effects of treatment for disease are sometimes labelled "iatrogenic;" the loss of hair from radiation treatment of cancer is often described in this way. As is true in the Gospels, the English derivatives from *therapeuo* are much more common; "therapy" and "therapeutic" are good examples.

When *iaomai* occurs in the third Gospel, we are able to see how uniquely Lukan it is. Matthew and Mark will use *therapeuo* to talk of healing or say nothing at all. One of the many examples of this occurs in Luke 5:17, where we are told that:

> On one of those days, as he was teaching, there were Pharisees and teachers of the law sitting by; who had come from every village of Galilee and Judea and Jerusalem; and the power of the Lord was with him to heal.''

This is Luke's introduction to the story of the healing of the paralytic, a story which also occurs in Matthew and Mark. In their introductions to the story, however, neither of our other angels include such a statement. (Matthew 9:1; Mark 2:1-2)

When Jesus commissions the twelve, Luke carefully distinguishes between the tasks of ''curing'' and ''healing:''

> And he called the twelve together and gave them power and authority over all demons and to cure diseases. And he sent them out to preach the kingdom of God and to heal. (Luke 9:1-2)

Mark says simply that Jesus ''began to send them out two by two and gave them authority over the unclean spirits.''   (Mark 6:7) Matthew also mentions the authority over unclean spirits, adding that the disciples have the authority '' . . . to cast them out and to cure every disease and infirmity.'' (Matthew 10:1)

All four Gospels contain the story of the slave in the Garden of Gethsemane whose ear is sliced off. It is our author alone who sets the situation right with the following: ''But Jesus said, 'No more of this!' And he touched his ear and healed him.'' (Luke 22:51)

Peter's words to Cornelius' household are a good summary with which to make our point:

> "Truly I perceive that God shows no partiality, but in every nation any one who fears him and does what is right is acceptable to him. You know the word which he sent to Israel, preaching good news of peace by Jesus Christ (he is the Lord of all), the word which was proclaimed throughout all Judea, beginning from Galilee after the baptism which John preached: how God anointed Jesus of Nazareth with the Holy Spirit and with power; how he went about doing good and healing all that were oppressed by the devil, for God was with him." (Acts 10:34-38)

Our angel says that "healing" and "curing" are *not* the same thing. At the same time, Luke says that "healing" and "setting things right" *are* the same. "Healing" is bringing together of things that belong together, the making whole of things rent apart. When "healing" occurs, Luke says, relationships or bodies are "set right."

The word for "right" in Greek is *dikaios*; it can also be translated as "innocent" or "just." When the centurion sees Jesus' body on the cross in the third Gospel, he says, "Certainly this man was *dikaios*." (Luke 23:47) In the words to Cornelius that we have just seen, Peter says that any one who fears God and does *"right"* is acceptable to God. (Acts 10:35) The words are the same. Somehow, we must be able to think as Luke does if we are to understand, for our English words of translation do not really say the same thing at all. When we think "right," the word "wrong" comes to mind; when we think "innocent," we hear "guilty" as its oppostie. When Luke hears *dikaios*, he hears God's voice speaking to Moses on the deliverance side of the Red Sea, "I am your healer."

We read the Bible together and ask our angels to hold our hands as we do so because we want to be able to hear their voices. We want to be able to hear God's words to Moses and Jesus' words with "ears that can hear," the kind of ears of which the prophet Isaiah speaks. This requires faithful communities in conversation; this requires time and talk and then patience and love. I am able to hear Luke hear God's voice to Moses because of Old Testament scholar Walter Brueggemann, actually, and this kind of conversation in community. We are part of a larger discussion about "justice" when I say that Luke thinks that "healing" and "justice" are the same thing. Walter, who dances the words of the Old Testament as I dance the words of the New, looks me straight in the eye and says, "Exodus 15." With this, everything in my head changes. I look at Exodus 15 and read the story all the way to its very end. Then I take a hard, long look at Luke and ask him, "Is this so?" And I see a smile on our angel's face and a bit of "at last" in his approval of "ears that can hear."

For the author of Luke-Acts, *healing* and *justice* are the same. When there is healing, things become *dikaios*; when justice is done, wholeness is the result. Healing and justice are God's work in creation; healing and justice are the work of the incarnate faithful in creation. Luke says that in the power of the Holy Spirit, "Jesus is *dikaios*; Jesus brings God and creation together again in love." Luke says that in the power of the Holy Spirit, the faithful who fear God, who do what is *dikaios* and call upon the name of Jesus are acceptable to God. The life and work of Jesus and the faithful who call upon his name bring God and creation together again in love.

We have to put Luke and Acts back-to-back in order to see its shape, in order to see our angel's "message" of justice and healing. And when we do this, Luke's

language of "power" and "authority" gives us Isaiah's
"eyes that can see, ears that can hear." We have already
noted that the Holy Spirit is the main character of
Luke-Acts, and we have already seen how the genealogy
divides Luke's story of Jesus' birth and baptism from
the rest of his life and work. Once we know this much
about the structure of Luke-Acts, we notice that the
language of "power" and "authority" emerges in Luke
4. We can illustrate Luke's use of this language as follows:

					God's Three Interventions
Luke 1-3	Luke 4:1-21:38	Evil 22 & 23	The Bridge Luke 24 Acts 1:11	Acts 2-10	Acts 11-28

Our angel tells us that on three occasions, God inter-
venes in human events with power and authority. The
first of these is in the inauguration of Jesus' ministry.
Jesus is led into and out of the wilderness by the power
of the Holy Spirit. In the desert, he is tempted by the
devil and Jesus withstands the temptations, the central
one of which is Satan's offer of all the authority and
the glory of "all the kingdoms of the world." (Luke
4:5-6) Because Jesus is full of the power of the Spirit
and able to withstand the temptations, the devil departs
from Jesus "until an opportune time." (Luke 4:13)

Jesus' ministry is free from evil. He teaches and heals
and celebrates table-fellowship. He commissions the

twelve and the seventy, giving them the same power and authority which God has bestowed upon him. The "opportune time" for the return of evil is in the passion; Satan is the first character named in Luke's story of Jesus' crucifixion and death. Our angel tells us that "Satan entered Judas Iscariot." (Luke 22:3) And only Luke among our four authors tells us that Satan is responsible for Peter's denial:

> "Simon, Simon, behold, Satan demanded to have you, that he might sift you like wheat, but I have prayed for you that you may not fail; and when you have turned again, strengthen your brethren." (Luke 22:31-32)

There is no mention of the power of the Holy Spirit in Luke's passion; it is a time when evil reigns in creation.

However, God will not have it be so and raises Jesus from the grave. The resurrection is God's second intervention in human history, and is—for Luke—a time in between times. Chapter 14 of the Gospel and Acts 1:1-14 are the center section, or the "bridge" of the two-volume work. In this "bridge," the empty tomb is discovered, Jesus appears to the faithful and ascends into heaven, leaving the faithful with this promise:

> "It is not for you to know times or seasons which the Father has fixed by his own authority. But you shall receive power when the Holy Spirit has come upon you; and you shall be my witnesses in Jerusalem and in all Judea and Samaria and to the end of the earth." (Acts 1:7-8)

The Holy Spirit is poured out upon the Jews in Acts 2 and upon the Gentiles in Cornelius' household in Acts 10. This is Jesus' promise; this is God's third and forever intervention into human events.

There is no evil, no mention of Satan in the "bridge"

section of Luke-Acts. In this second of three divine interventions, God completely overturns the death that the power of evil has caused. When the Holy Spirit is poured out upon the world, however, it is clear that evil is not vanquished forever. The opposition that the faithful in Acts encounter suggests that the devil's claim in Luke 4:4-5 is still true. To some degree, evil has authority in "all the kingdoms of the world." However, in the light of the resurrection and the power of the Holy Spirit, God's power and authority are great enough to begin to heal the world.

Luke's two-volume work has no ending. We wonder how this can be when we remember that it is Luke who gives us the most clear and careful literary introduction in the New Testament. The book of Acts closes with Paul under house arrest in Rome, "preaching the kingdom of God and teaching about the Lord Jesus Christ quite openly and unhindered." (Acts 28:31) Our angel thinks that this is as good a place as any to stop. Luke knows that the healing of creation has begun but is not yet complete.

Luke knows that once the Holy Spirit has been poured out upon all the world, one can pick up the story of the healing of creation almost anywhere. The story of Paul's journeys that our author chooses to tell is the first of the stories of the faithful that can be told through time until our time. Where the book of Acts ends, the story of the rest of the church begins.

"Here is the truth, the *asphaleia* about what you have heard," our angel says. "God's power and presence in the world through the person of Jesus of Nazareth and in the Holy Spirit are God's promise come true. 'I am your healer,' says the Lord your God. And so it is to this very day.''

Ninety-nine generations later, we are to do as Luke instructs his own community. We are to devote ourselves to the apostles' teaching, to fellowship, to the breaking of bread and to the prayers. The hand that Luke holds out to us assures us that through our lives in faithful community and in the name of the risen Christ, justice will be known in creation and that Creator and creation will come together in love. ''Surely, this is right,'' we pray. Amen.

Conclusion

Matthew, Mark, Luke and John,
Guard the bed I lie upon;
Four pillars round my bed,
Four angels round my head.

One to watch, one to pray,
And two to keep me till the day.

As we have begun, so we close in prayer. We are blessed in the richness of our traditions, the differences among the Gospels. We have John with whom to pray, with whom to learn something new about "signs" and the ways in which we may recognize God in the world around us. We have Mark with whom we watch; Mark who reminds us of the immediacy of the "good news" and the urgency with which we are to live in God's kingdom. We have the wise hand of Matthew the teacher, the one who leads us forward to teach others at the same time that he holds us to our Jewish roots. We have the hand of Luke, who shows us a Jesus and a church who are God's instruments of healing and justice in creation.

Certainly, the evangelists have become our "angels." They are God's messengers for their own communities and their own times; they are God's messengers in our time. They have also become our "guardians" as well. They are the keepers of our Christian heritage and tradition. They are the hands we hold as we reach out toour faithful forebears. And they offer us their hands as we reach out to Jesus.

Matthew, Mark, Luke and John—our angels serve God and serve God's holy people, the church. As we hold their hands, they also lead us out in faith to serve. It is our fourth of the four who reminds us of the servanthood to which we are called. It is Luke who tells us that as the power of evil grows strong in the world, Jesus leaves the disciples with this reminder:

> " . . . let the greatest among you become as the youngest, and the leader as one who serves. For which is the greater, the one who sits at table, or one who serves? Is it not the one who sits at table? But I am among you as one who serves." (Luke 22:26-27)

And so we pray—with four to keep us till the day. Amen.

Appendix
Questions for Discussion

Chapter 2
"In the Beginning Was the Word"

1. Were we to write a Gospel, what would it look like?

2. We must begin our own story somewhere. Where would that be? What would we call this beginning?

3. What stories from the Old Testament hold the most meaning for our story as the community of the faithful?

4. With which biblical stories do we have trouble in our time? Why is this so?

5. How do we recognize the *Logos* in our time?

Chapter 3
"One to Pray"

1. What events in your life brought you to faith through "seeing is believing"?

2. What events in your life sustained this faith?

3. John mentions "memory" and "remembrance" on several occasions. How does memory work for faith? What is memory's value for faith?

4. What are the "signs" of the presence of God's Spirit among us today?

5. Suppose that John is writing his Gospel for a community in our time. What other images would complete Jesus' "I am . . . " sayings?

Chapter 4
"One to Watch"

1. What is of "immediate" concern for our community?

2. What in our lives do we need "to watch"?

3. Mark suggests that life and death are known together, that as he goes toward death, Jesus brings life. Where can we see life in death this way?

4. How have we experienced God's forgiveness even when we have fled in fear?

5. Jesus promises that when we are in adversity, the Holy Spirit will speak through us. Have we experienced this in our own lives?

Chapter 5
"Matthew the Teacher"

1. What responsibilities do we have for teaching and instruction as the *ekklesia*, the ones whom God calls out?

2. In our "treasure" that is the church, what do we take out that is new and that is old in our time?

3. How might we fashion a contemporary genealogy for our own church community? Whose names and what stories would we include?

4. In what Old Testament passages do we see the story of Jesus foretold? Where do we see God's promises and how have they come true?

5. What of Jesus' teaching would we include in a "manual" for others? Would this be the same if we were to seal the manual in a time capsule?

Chapter 6
"Luke the Healer"

1. What needs to be "cured" so that "healing" can happen? What needs to be "fixed" so that "justice" may occur?

2. Where can we see healing and justice where there is also disease and brokenness?

3. What do "eyes that can see" and "ears that can hear" look like for us? What do we see and hear anew?

4. The "apostles' teaching" that Luke mentions in Acts 2:42 have become our traditions. What of these should we study?

5. We are to be like Jesus, Luke says. How does this feel? What might we do differently from now on?